FOOTBALL'S
GREATEST
RIVALRIES

Written by Andy Greeves

Designed by Adam Wilsher

ASPEN
BOOKS

© 2022. Published by Aspen Books, an imprint of Pillar Box Red Publishing Ltd. Printed in India.

ISBN: 978-1-914536-30-4

CONTENTS

EUROPE

REST OF THE WORLD

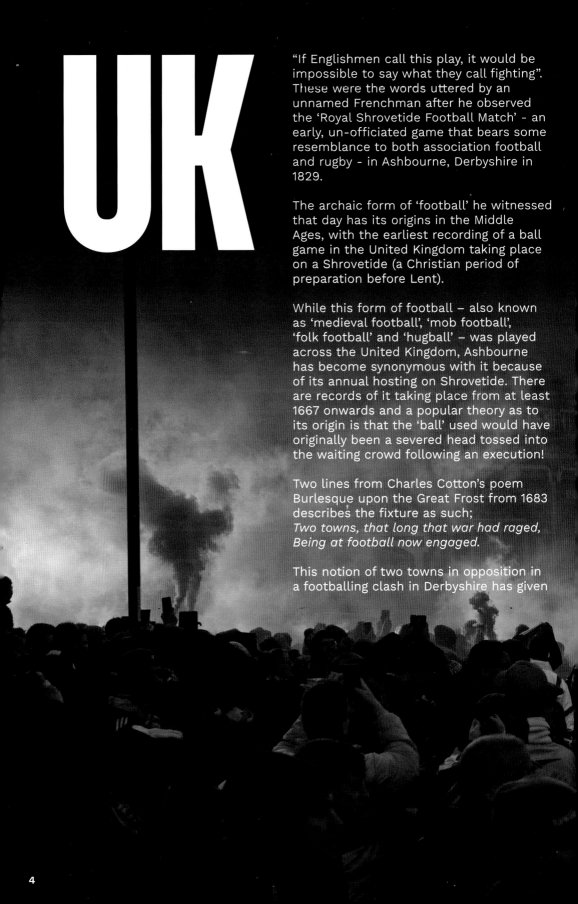

UK

"If Englishmen call this play, it would be impossible to say what they call fighting". These were the words uttered by an unnamed Frenchman after he observed the 'Royal Shrovetide Football Match' - an early, un-officiated game that bears some resemblance to both association football and rugby - in Ashbourne, Derbyshire in 1829.

The archaic form of 'football' he witnessed that day has its origins in the Middle Ages, with the earliest recording of a ball game in the United Kingdom taking place on a Shrovetide (a Christian period of preparation before Lent).

While this form of football – also known as 'medieval football', 'mob football', 'folk football' and 'hugball' – was played across the United Kingdom, Ashbourne has become synonymous with it because of its annual hosting on Shrovetide. There are records of it taking place from at least 1667 onwards and a popular theory as to its origin is that the 'ball' used would have originally been a severed head tossed into the waiting crowd following an execution!

Two lines from Charles Cotton's poem Burlesque upon the Great Frost from 1683 describes the fixture as such;
Two towns, that long that war had raged, Being at football now engaged.

This notion of two towns in opposition in a footballing clash in Derbyshire has given rise to the idea that the term 'derby' - describing two rival football clubs going head-to-head – derives from the county in which the Royal Shrovetide Football Match took - and, to this day, takes - place.

Another theory is that the term 'derby' originates from 'The Derby' – a horse race which was founded by Edward Smith-Stanley, the 12th Earl of Derby, and has been staged at Epsom Downs Racecourse in Surrey, England since 1780. The term 'derby' is understood to have been used as a noun in English since 1840 to describe a sporting encounter.

With it widely accepted the term 'derby' comes from the United Kingdom (whichever theory you choose to believe!), it seems fitting the first such match – indeed the first-ever football fixture with rules (the so-called 'Sheffield Rules') took place in England. The 'Rules derby' saw Sheffield FC – the world's first football club – beat near-neighbours Hallam FC by two goals to nil on the 26th of December 1860. The world's first international also took place in the United Kingdom as Scotland drew 0-0 with England on the 30th of November 1872.

The United Kingdom is also home to the oldest football league in the world with The Football League (now The English Football League or EFL) staging its first season in 1888/89.

With such history, many footballing rivalries in the United Kingdom pre-date those around the rest of the world. From the top of the professional game in England, Wales, Scotland and Northern Ireland down to non-League level, there are countless club rivalries the length and breadth of the country. As we will discover throughout this book, the reasons two clubs – and specifically, their supporters - have such rivalries is often as diverse and shrouded in mystery as the origin of the term 'derby' itself.

There are thousands of derby matches we could have covered, but this section looks at four particularly fiery affairs, including the so-called 'Old Firm' clash involving Glaswegian giants Celtic and Rangers, and the Manchester United-Liverpool rivalry in the North West of England.

One of the clubs covered in this section doesn't even play in the top two divisions of their domestic league at the time of writing; proof that in the United Kingdom, a club's divisional status at any particular time is no indicator as to just how ferocious a rivalry they can have with another.

THE NORTH WEST DERBY

Liverpool vs Manchester United

Separated by a distance of just over 30 miles, the civic rivalry between two of England's great northern powerhouses, Liverpool and Manchester, pre-dates their footballing animosities.

Liverpool put itself firmly on the map in 1715 with the opening of the world's first commercial wet dock while Manchester's significant role in the industrial revolution saw it grow to become the most productive cotton spinning town in the world, with 108 mills, by 1853.

Manchester's mills imported raw cotton from the West Indies and southern states of America through the Port of Liverpool. The Liverpool and Manchester Railway opened in 1830 with the primary objective of moving raw materials and finished goods – as well as passengers – between the Port of Liverpool and Manchester's mills and factories.

While the shipping and cotton industries coexisted harmoniously for many decades, the

construction of the Manchester Ship Canal between 1887 and 1894 served as an incendiary moment in Manchester and Liverpool's future relationship. The canal gave ocean-going vessels direct access to Manchester and bypassed the Port of Liverpool in the process. It was funded by Manchester's merchants after they had become frustrated with the charges imposed on the transportation of their goods by the Port of Liverpool and the Liverpool to Manchester Railway during a period known as the 'Long Depression'. Liverpool's politicians, as well as the Mersey Docks and Harbour Board, opposed the building of the canal, but eventually Manchester's industrialists were able to purchase a corridor of land from the Wirral to Salford in order to execute their plan.

In 1894, the year the Manchester Ship Canal opened, English football's two most successful teams met for the first time, as Liverpool faced Newton Heath (now Manchester United) in

a Football League test match. By virtue of their 2-0 win at Blackburn Rovers' Ewood Park ground that day, Liverpool were elected to Division One for the 1894/95 season while Newton Heath were invited to Division Two.

Liverpool became Champions of England for the first time in 1901 and collected their second title in 1905/06 while the newly-named Manchester United joined the top flight for the first time in 1906/07. The following season, the Red Devils were Division One Champions for the first time and followed up that success by claiming the FA Cup in 1909 and a second league title in 1910/11. Between the end of World War I and the start of World War II, Liverpool became league champions in 1922 and 1923, while United endured three relegations to Division Two and three subsequent promotions back to the top flight.

After World War II it was the arrival of a former Liverpool captain, Matt Busby, who transformed United from being a yo-yo team to a major footballing force. Busby's United won five league titles between 1945 and 1969, as well as two FA Cups and the European Cup in 1968. Over at Anfield, Bill Shankly created a similar dynasty with Liverpool, who were promoted back to the top flight in 1962 and then won three league titles and two FA Cups as well as the UEFA Cup between 1959 and 1974.

The Busby-Shankly era saw United and Liverpool go head-to-head for major honours on a regular basis. Results of the matches between the two clubs became more important in the pursuit of major honours – Liverpool's home and away wins over United during the 1963/64 season to clinch the title from the Red Devils by four points being a real case in point. While they were in competition for leagues and cups, the fixture still perhaps lacked the real, deep-lying rivalry of say the Old Firm derby or North London derby. Indeed, one could

even question whether Liverpool-United could be described as a derby when that term in British football had typically been reserved for inter-city clashes.

Speaking to BBC Football back in December 2014, football sociologist John Williams claimed that Liverpool-United, "became much more poisonous... in the late 1970s and early 1980s, partially for football reasons but also because of external influence.

"There was a perception in Liverpool that their hugely successful but 'professional', 'workman-like' teams were always somehow in the shadow of the stars at Old Trafford - the derisory United nickname in Liverpool at the time was 'The Glams'.

"Because Everton and Liverpool were 'friendly' rivals - people in the same families on different sides and with no geographical territorial divide - when things properly kicked off the Reds needed a better local target than the Blues could provide."

Williams said it was "quite hard" for Liverpool and Everton fans to generate "authentic and satisfying feelings of hatred" while Manchester City seemed "unlikely rivals" to Manchester United supporters; "The bogeyman for each club seemed obvious and to lie at the opposite end of the M62: an unbearable smugness at all-conquering Liverpool and a perceived arrogance at underachieving United."

The 1970s was a decade when Liverpool reigned supreme, winning four league titles, two European Cups, two UEFA Cups, the FA Cup and the European Super Cup. After their last league title in 1967, United wouldn't become Champions of England again until 1992 and suffered the indignity of relegation to Division Two in 1974, before returning to the top flight a year later. It was around this period of Liverpool domination and United struggle that Williams suggests the Red Devils were, "media darlings who got far too much publicity".

United were at least deserving of their publicity when they won their first major cup final against Liverpool in 1977. Goals from Stuart Pearson and Jimmy Greenhoff gave them a 2-1 victory in that year's FA Cup Final. With the Merseysiders having won the league title and European Cup that season, the Red Devils' cup final victory prevented Liverpool from achieving a unique treble.

Liverpool won four consecutive League Cups at the start of the 1980s and gained revenge for 1977, with a 2-1 extra-time triumph over United in the 1983 League Cup Final. The Merseysiders claimed two league titles, two FA Cups and two European Cups during the decade as the managerial baton at Anfield passed from Bob Paisley to Joe Fagan and then on to legendary former player, Kenny Dalglish. United collected two FA Cups during the same period. En route to their victory over Everton in the 1985 final, United faced Liverpool in a Goodison Park semi-final and Maine Road replay, with both matches overshadowed by violent scenes.

The mid-to-late 1980s was a difficult period for English football. Rioting prior to Liverpool's 1985 European Cup Final against Juventus led to the death of 39 supporters while 97 fans died as a result of overcrowding on the Leppings Lane terrace during an FA Cup semi-final against Nottingham Forest at Hillsborough in 1989. False media stories, supplied by the South Yorkshire Police, suggesting that hooliganism and drunkenness by Liverpool supporters had caused the Hillsborough disaster contributed to the long and agonising wait for the families to get some form of justice, after the initial coroner's inquest, completed in 1991, ruled all the deaths accidental. The second coroner's inquests, held between 2014 and 2016, ruled the supporters were unlawfully killed due to grossly negligent failures by police and ambulance services to fulfil their duty of care.

The vicious nature of the Liverpool-Manchester United rivalry has, on occasion, seen elements of both clubs' supporter base sink to the lowest possible depths as they have taunted opposing fans with chants relating to both Hillsborough and the 1958 Munich air disaster. The latter saw 23 passengers lose their lives when British European Airways Flight 609 crashed on its third attempt to take off from a snow-covered runway at Munich-Riem Airport in West Germany. The plane was carrying the Manchester United team, officials, supporters and journalists from a European Cup match in Belgrade to Manchester, via a refuelling in Munich. Eight United players were amongst the dead.

Sir Matt Busby, who had been onboard that flight in 1958 as United manager, was at Old Trafford on the 3rd of May 1993 as the Red Devils ended a 26-year wait for a league title, by getting their hands on the inaugural Premier League trophy. Liverpool endured a greater interlude for their next title – becoming Champions of England for the first time in 30 years in 2020. During that period, between 1990 and 2020, United – under the management of the legendary Sir Alex Ferguson - won 13 league titles, 23 domestic cups and five European trophies. This

"My greatest challenge is not what's happening at the moment, my greatest challenge was knocking Liverpool right off their f***ing perch. And you can print that."

- Sir Alex Ferguson

included the Premier League, FA Cup and European Cup 'treble' in 1999.

Liverpool remained hot on United's heels for much of this period, winning three FA Cups, four League Cups, two European Cups, the UEFA Cup, three UEFA Super Cups and one FIFA Club World Cup. But during the Ferguson era at Old Trafford between 1986 and 2013, Liverpool relinquished their status as English football's top dogs to their big rivals. There were two cup finals between the sides during this period with United winning the 1996 FA Cup Final while Liverpool came out on top in the 2003 League Cup Final.

In 2009, United equalled Liverpool's record of 18 top flight English league titles and surpassed it with another triumph in 2011. As the Red Devils were in the midst of a golden period in their club's history, a banner displayed by Liverpool at Anfield during a Reds-United match in 1994 read 'AU REVIOUR [ERIC] CANTONA AND MAN. UNITED... COME BACK WHEN YOU'VE WON 18 [TITLES]'. Proving that football fans rarely forget, United supporters headed to Anfield during the 2009/10 season with a banner of their own that read 'YOU TOLD US TO COME BACK WHEN WE'VE WON 18... WE ARE BACK'.

After a 1-1 draw between Liverpool and Manchester United at Old Trafford in October 2011, United left-back Patrice Evra complained to the match referee that Reds striker Luis Suárez had used racist language against him. Suárez was handed an eight-game ban and a £40,000 fine, pending an appeal. Liverpool initially defended Suárez's innocence, with the club's players even wearing T-shirts in support of the Uruguayan prior to a match against Wigan Athletic. In January 2012, after reviewing a 115-page document released by the Football Association - detailing the case and the reasons for the punishment they awarded - Liverpool confirmed they would not appeal. In Suárez's second game back after his ban, he started for the Reds in an away game at Manchester United. Prior to kick-off, Suárez refused

to shake hands with Evra. The United player responded by celebrating in front of him after United's 2-1 win that day.

Jamie Carragher, who was a Liverpool player during that time, has since claimed his former club, "got it massively wrong" in response to Evra's claims telling Sky Sports in 2019 that they made, "a massive mistake" in such public support of Suárez.

Liverpool and Manchester United's rivalry was played out on the European stage for the first time, as the Merseysiders triumphed 3-1 on aggregate in a UEFA Europa League round of 16 tie in 2016. Liverpool have enjoyed the better record in the recent head-to-head meetings, with results including

a 5-0 Premier League win at Old Trafford in October 2021. Under the management of Jürgen Klopp, the Merseysiders also appear better placed to win major honours currently.

While Liverpool are in the ascendency right now, the pendulum of power has tilted between these great adversaries on many occasions over the decades. This rivalry is often the measure of the age-old debate of who the biggest club in England is. As of March 2022, United had one more title (19) than Liverpool (18) and one more trophy overall (66 to Liverpool's 65 – including their 2022 League Cup success), meaning – as ever – there is very little to separate the jewels in English football's crown.

THE NORTH LONDON DERBY

Arsenal vs Tottenham Hotspur

London boasts more professional football clubs than any other city in the world, with 13 teams plying their trade in the top four divisions of English league football as of the start of the 2021/22 season. With several dozen semi-professional clubs and hundreds of amateur teams too, rarely does a day pass during the football season without some form of derby match taking place in the capital.

While Chelsea have been London's most successful club of the past few decades, Arsenal versus Tottenham Hotspur has, historically at least, been the capital's biggest and most important fixture.

Like so many derbies covered in this book, the north London derby has humble beginnings. Indeed, when the teams first met for a friendly match on 19th of November 1887, neither side was even technically from London! Then known as 'Royal Arsenal', the Gunners – who were formed just a year earlier - were located in Plumstead, which was then part of Kent. Tottenham, which has been a municipal borough since 1934 and part of the London Borough of Haringey since 1963, was located within the historic

county of Middlesex at the time. Tottenham Hotspur were founded as 'Hotspur Football Club' in 1882 by a group of local schoolboys, with their current name being adopted two years later. Spurs hosted the first 'north London derby' on Tottenham Marshes back in 1887 and were leading 2-1 in the match with around 15 minutes remaining when it was abandoned due to poor light.

Arsenal became the first club from the south of England to join the Football League in 1893 and reached the top flight by 1904. They were joined in the old First Division by Spurs in 1909, with the first competitive clash between the pair ending in a 1-0 win for the team known as 'Woolwich Arsenal' by that point on 4th of December that year.

In the early years, Arsenal versus Spurs was nothing more than a local derby. In 1913 however, a major rivalry was born...

The Gunners' decision to move north of the Thames from their Manor Ground home in Plumstead to a new stadium in Highbury – just four miles from Tottenham – was resented by Spurs. While Arsenal allowed the Lilywhites to use their new home ground during part of World War I, when White Hart Lane was temporarily set up as a munition factory, the ill feeling between the clubs soon intensified.

Prior to the start of the 1919/20 season – and the resumption of league football in England for the first time since 1914/15 – the Football League opted to expand the First Division from 20 to 22 teams. Chelsea, who had finished 19th in the division in 1914/15 and would have been relegated in usual circumstances, were allowed to maintain their place in the top flight. A vote was cast on who would take the final spot in the division.

Having been a member of the First Division before the war – albeit the team who finished bottom of the league – a strong argument could be made for Spurs, like Chelsea, to stay in the division. Barnsley, who came third in Division Two behind promoted sides Derby County and Preston North End, seemed like the other logical choice. But five other teams - Arsenal, Birmingham City, Hull City, Nottingham Forest and Wolverhampton Wanderers put forward their case. In the end, it was decided Arsenal – despite only finishing sixth (later discovered to be fifth due to an error in the calculation of goal difference) in Division Two in 1914/15 – would be promoted and Tottenham relegated. Spurs returned to the top flight in

1920/21 and won 2-1 in the first clash of the rivals since the controversial vote. The increasing ill-feeling between the clubs manifested on the pitch in a league match the following campaign. In its coverage of the Gunners' 2-1 win at Tottenham on 23rd of September 1922, the Sunday Evening Telegraph wrote: "After the Spurs goal came the most disgraceful scene I have witnessed on any ground at any time. The players pulled the referee, blows with fists were exchanged, and all the dignity that appertains in the referee was rudely trampled on."

A Football Association Commission of Inquiry was held on 5th of October 1922 to investigate the match politely dubbed: "An amazingly strenuous contest" by The Sportsman newspaper. After hearing evidence from the officials and players of both clubs, Spurs player Bert Smith was suspended for a month for having used 'filthy language' while the Gunners' Alex Graham and Stephen Dunn were also reprimanded for their part in the White Hart Lane fracas.

Arsenal won five Division One titles between 1931 and the outbreak of World War II in 1939, while Spurs yo-yoed between the top flight and second tier during this period. The Lilywhites repaid a debt of gratitude to their rivals during the war, allowing the Gunners to play at White Hart Lane after Arsenal Stadium was requisitioned by the government as an Air Raid Precaution centre.

The Gunners' success continued when football resumed after World War II, with further title successes in 1948 and 1953. But Spurs, who won their first top-flight title in 1951, were the dominant force in north London during the 1960s, becoming the first English team of the 20th century to win both the league and the FA Cup in a single season in 1960/61. Bill Nicholson's 'double' winners also

became the first British side to collect a major continental trophy as they lifted the European Cup Winners' Cup in 1963. They also won the FA Cup in 1962 and 1967. Arsenal's response to Spurs' achievements came with a double of their own in 1970/71. They wrapped up the league title with a 1-0 triumph at White Hart Lane on 3rd of May 1971.

"When I was playing for Tottenham, the Arsenal-Spurs rivalry was so strong. We couldn't even wear red. The passions between the two clubs... we couldn't put on a red tie or drive a red car"

– Osvaldo Ardiles

Ray Kennedy scored for the Gunners in front of a crowd of 51,992, with an estimated 50,000-plus spectators locked outside the ground. Spurs won two League Cups and the UEFA Cup during the 1970s, prior to relegation to Division Two in 1977 and a return to the top flight a year later. The Gunners collected the FA Cup in 1979.

It was during this decade that a seemingly unthinkable ground-sharing proposal was reported. The Daily Express newspaper of 26th of November 1977 led with a headline of 'Arsenal Hotspurs!' as they revealed potential plans for a 75,000-seater stadium to be built at Alexandra Palace, which would be home to "London's Big Two". By early 1979, such ideas had been quashed, with Horace Cutler, leader of the Greater London Council, surmising: "The reaction of local residents and local politicians of all parties was instantaneous, and totally adverse."

Back-to-back FA Cup successes in 1981 and 1982 and a second UEFA Cup triumph in 1984 saw bragging rights in north London go to Tottenham in the first half of the 1980s before returning to Arsenal when they won the First Division in 1988/89. Two seasons later, the Gunners were closing in on the league

title once again when they met Spurs, who were in the midst of a troubling financial period, in an FA Cup semi-final. Such was the demand for tickets for the match on 14th of April 1991, the Football Association broke with previous tradition and allowed a last-four tie to be held at Wembley Stadium for the first time.

A thunderous free-kick from Paul Gascoigne and a brace from Gary Lineker gave underdogs Spurs a 3-1 triumph on the day. They subsequently went on to win the FA Cup that season with a 2-1 extra-time victory over Nottingham Forest in the final. Arsenal mirrored this achievement in 1993 – beating Spurs 1-0 in an FA Cup semi-final at Wembley before going on to lift the trophy. George Graham's Gunners also won the League Cup in 1992/93.

A seminal moment in the modern history of both Arsenal and the north London derby came in 1996 with the Gunners' appointment of Arsene Wenger. The Frenchman went on to guide Arsenal to three Premier League titles and seven FA Cups, which included two seasons they won the double (1997/98 and 2001/02) and another in which they went an entire campaign unbeaten in the league, being dubbed the 'Invincibles' by the British tabloid press in the process. As they

had done in 1971, Arsenal confirmed one of their league title successes at White Hart Lane, this time with a 2-2 draw with Tottenham on 25th of April 2004. It was a painful period for Spurs supporters, who endured mid-table finishes while world stars such as Thierry Henry, Patrick Vieira and Dennis Bergkamp turned out for their sworn enemies. To make matters worse, Tottenham club captain Sol Campbell allowed his contract to run down at White Hart Lane before departing on a free transfer and subsequently signing for Arsenal in the summer of 2001. An act of treachery in the hearts and minds of Tottenham supporters, Campbell was treated to a hostile reception on his first return to N17 in November 2001 for a Premier League match that ended in a 1-1 draw.

In the years leading up to Wenger's departure from Arsenal in 2018 and since, the pendulum of power in north London has swung slightly in favour of Spurs. Having finished above Arsenal for five consecutive seasons between 2017 and 2021, the Lilywhites have ended Gunners' fans tradition of 'St Totteringham's Day' – which took place annually between 1996 and 2017 when it became mathematically impossible for Spurs to finish above their local rivals.

While Tottenham fans have enjoyed superior league finishes and a run to the UEFA Champions League Final in 2019, Arsenal followers will point to the fact the Lilywhites have won nothing since 2008 while they have collected four FA Cups in the same period.

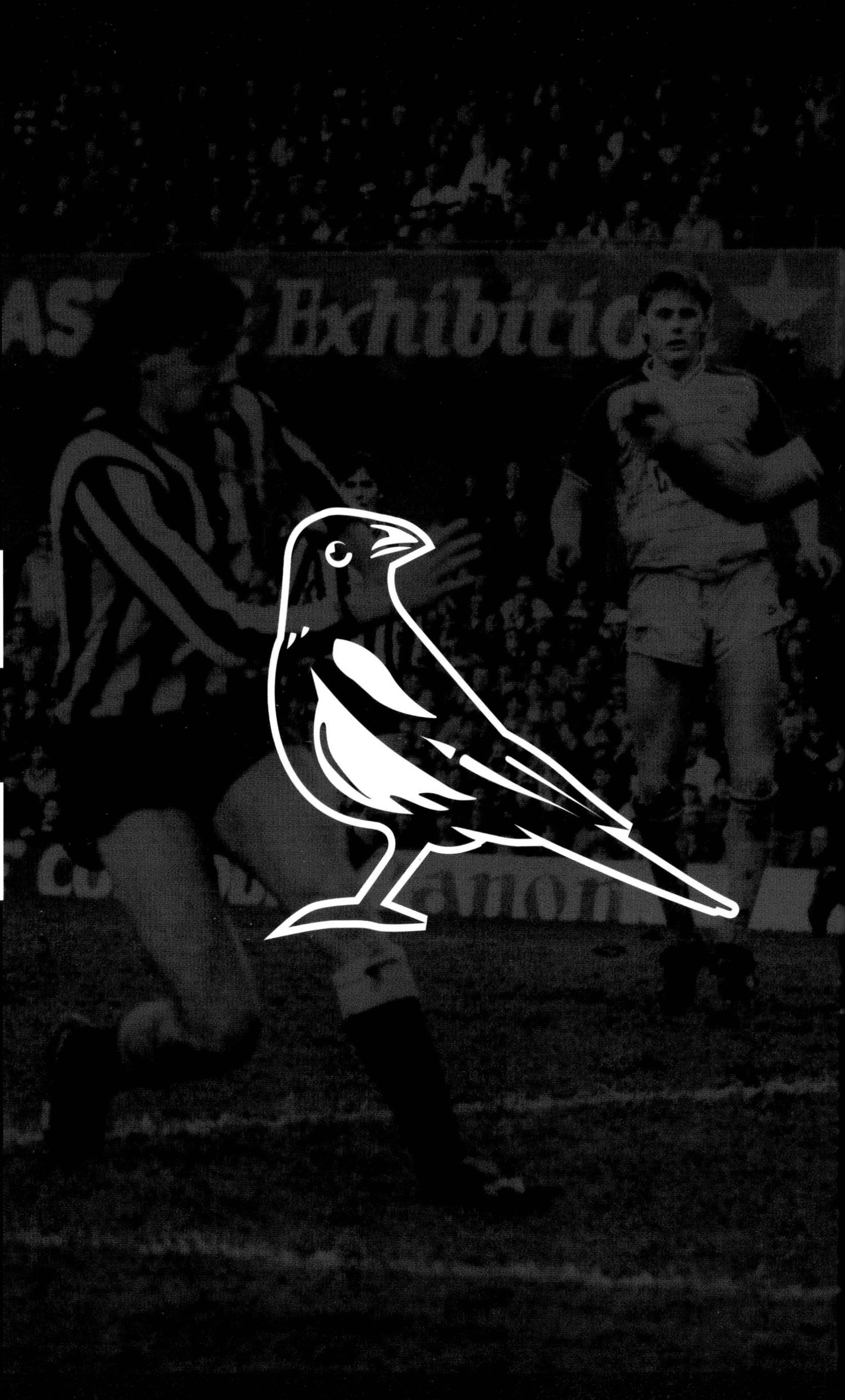

THE TYNE-WEAR DERBY

Newcastle vs Sunderland
Contribution by Rob Mason

The North-East of England views itself as a 'hot-bed of football' but, to a certain extent, its clubs are ignored by most of the rest of the country. Geographically isolated, unless they are playing each other, the two regional giants of Sunderland and Newcastle United have to travel much longer distances than fans of other clubs in England. Black Cats supporters had to travel further than any other club to attend their league fixtures in 2021/22 while members of the 'Toon Army' weren't far behind in terms of the number of miles they racked up during the same campaign. Both teams command phenomenal support away as well as at home regardless of an almost complete absence of success in the modern era.

Sunderland's last major trophy was the FA Cup – won as a Second Division side in 1973 - while Newcastle last claimed major silverware in 1969 in the shape of the old Inter-Cities Fairs Cup. Despite this, Newcastle frequently pull in crowds of over 50,000 while Sunderland – relegated from the Premier League to League One in consecutive seasons in

33

2017 and 2018 – command bigger crowds in their fourth successive season in the third tier than many clubs in the Premier League. After half a century without a trophy, this is an impressive feat.

Without Premier League titles, European trophies or major domestic cups to sustain them, the regional bragging rights of being 'Cock 'o the North' therefore rest on the outcome of the Wear-Tyne derby. As this book has outlined, most derbies are between teams within the same city. Rivalries such as Liverpool and Manchester United are big games between hugely successful clubs, but each also has a significant rival within their own city which means their meetings are not their only derbies of the season. In contrast, on the day the fixtures come out – when the clubs are in the same division at least - there is only one question that Sunderland and

Newcastle fans have in mind: 'when do we play Newcastle/Sunderland?'

When derby matches come around the history and rivalry of the region come to the fore. Sunderland v Newcastle derbies are not two teams from the same city squabbling over who is the better football team, they are expressions of pride in where people come from with the added twist of that historical aggravation running back centuries. Rivalry between the cities goes back centuries. Sunderland sees itself as the poor relation in terms of how the cities are viewed, but absolutely not the poor relation in football terms. In 1610, following a petition from the City of Newcastle, King James I ruled that some of Sunderland's revenue from coal must be paid to Newcastle merchants. It was a decision that did not go down well in Sunderland and sowed the seeds of the modern-day

rivalry between those from the banks of the rivers Wear and Tyne. When Charles I, who succeeded James I, consistently awarded East of England Coal Trade Rights to Tyneside rather than Wearside, it added to the feeling in Sunderland that they were not being treated fairly. In the English Civil War of the 1600s, Sunderland and Newcastle took different sides. While Newcastle supported the Crown, Sunderland sided with Oliver Cromwell's Parliamentarians and offered no opposition to a Scottish army who camped at Sunderland from 1644 to 1647, defeating the Marquis of Newcastle's Royalist forces in a series of local battles. These events are still commemorated on a blue plaque on Wearmouth Bridge near the Stadium of Light.

As Richard Stonehouse, writing in The Guardian back in 2005, pointed out; "The Tyne-Wear derby may be perceived by the uninitiated as parochial and unsophisticated, but like the world's greatest derbies it has a historical conflict as its bedrock. And if anything, the Sunderland-Newcastle derby is the most legitimate conflict anywhere. A purposeful enmity if ever there was one. Unlike rivalries between other clubs, the differences between Newcastle and Sunderland date back to fighting based on the necessity to live and feed one's children, and benefit one's city."

In modern times, despite the two cities now both being part of the same county after the creation of Tyne & Wear in 1974, Wearsiders still feel priority is given to Tyneside. In 1980 the Tyneside Metro opened, serving only Tyneside although Wearside people had had to pay towards it. It took over two decades to be extended to Sunderland and even then, it only just reached Wearside. It still does not connect the city in anything like the way it does in Newcastle.

With the local BBC station being called BBC Newcastle and the ITV region being Tyne-Tees, Wearsiders constantly feel overlooked, while Tynesiders tend to see the near neighbours – the cities are 10 miles apart – as upstarts.

Sunderland are the older of the two clubs and are the most successful in terms of top-flight league titles won – six to Newcastle's four. At no time in history have Newcastle held as many league titles as Sunderland, although Newcastle have won the FA Cup more times – six to Sunderland's two. With Newcastle's newfound wealth having been taken over by Saudi Arabia backed owners after years of financial restriction under Mike Ashley, they may go on to finally overtake their rivals - but will have to win the Premier League three times to do so.

The first meeting of the two clubs took place on the 3rd of November 1883 when Sunderland beat Newcastle United's forerunners Newcastle East End 3-0 in a friendly on Tyneside. There were four more friendlies before the first major competitive meeting, almost exactly five years after the initial clash. On that occasion at Sunderland's Newcastle Road ground, Sunderland won 2-0 in a qualifying game for the English (FA) Cup; the world's oldest football competition,

created by Sunderland-born C.W. Alcock. However, having progressed Sunderland then resigned from the competition once they were drawn against short-lived local rivals Sunderland Albion, Sunderland not wanting to provide their (embryonic) near-neighbours with the cash boost a cup-tie between the clubs would provide. Sunderland Albion didn't survive beyond 1892 by which time Sunderland had joined the Football League and won it.

The same year saw the creation of Newcastle United when Newcastle East End joined forces with Newcastle West End. As Newcastle United, the Tynesiders

first met Sunderland in a friendly at St. James' Park on the 25th of February 1893 with the Black Cats winning 6-1, Johnny Campbell scoring four times for Sunderland who were en route to retaining the Football League title.

On Christmas Eve 1898 the clubs first met in the Football League, with Newcastle winning 3-2 at Sunderland's former Roker Park ground. Oddly, it took until the 10th league meeting for either team to win at home, when the Magpies came out on top with a 1-0 win at St. James' Park on the 25th of April 1903. The result denied Sunderland the chance to retain the league title they had won for a

fourth time in 1902. Showing that it is not just in modern times that people in the rest of the country fail to understand the rivalry between black and white and red and white, The Football Association sent representatives to monitor the match in case Newcastle let their neighbours win. Fat chance. There was no remote possibility of that and at the final whistle the home fans began immediate gloating as a brass band struck up 'Cock o' the North' before the teams had even left the pitch. A couple of years earlier, a Good Friday game at the same ground had been abandoned when a full-scale riot broke out; goal-posts and the club flag

were torn down as police resorted to wielding one of the net poles and wooden stakes as they tried to force fans back. The game was called off without a ball being kicked but the 'fistic encounters' as they were described at the time lasted for two hours before the ground was cleared.

Five years after Sunderland lost their 1903 title chance on Tyneside, Newcastle were enjoying a rich period in their history and en route to their third league title in five years when the clubs met at St. James' on the 5th of December 1908. With Sunderland leading 1-0 Newcastle equalised on the stroke of half time with a hotly-disputed penalty. Sunderland were so furious that they came out for the second half and scored eight times without reply to register a 9-1 away win that remained the highest top flight away win in England until Leicester City's 9-0 win at Southampton in 2019 (although Wolverhampton Wanderers also won 9-1 at Cardiff City in 1955).

There continued to be many hotly contested encounters, not least in 1913 when the clubs met in an FA Cup quarter-final that went to two replays before Sunderland won and went on to the final in a season where they were also league champions for a fifth time. For the second replay, Harry Low – whose brother Wilf played for Newcastle and was a Scotland international –

chose to play for Sunderland having been selected by Scotland. He never got another chance to represent his country and remained uncapped.

The inter-war years saw the teams' rivalry undimmed, although Newcastle were in the Second Division in the mid-thirties when Sunderland won their sixth league title and first FA Cup in 1936 and 37.

later in the return fixture as Newcastle made it a happy Christmas for their fans by winning 3-1, but when the sides met later in the season at St. James' in an FA Cup quarter-final, Holden scored twice as Sunderland won 2-0 to end United's cup reign. To date Newcastle haven't won a major domestic trophy since.

Both clubs continued to have their derby highs and lows: in 1979 Gary Rowell scored Sunderland's last derby hat-trick in a 4-1 win at Newcastle, while in 2010 Kevin Nolan scored three in a 5-1 United win at the same ground. In between, Ruud Gullit was sacked as Newcastle manager following a 2-1 home defeat to newly-promoted Sunderland when he preferred inexperienced youngster Paul Robinson to star striker Alan Shearer.

The most recent derby to date took place in March 2016, a 1-1 draw at St. James that ended a run of six successive Sunderland victories – the longest such run in Wear-Tyne derby history. With that run preceded by two draws, Newcastle are winless in the last nine derbies. The fixture has been paused since Newcastle's relegation in 2016 and with Sunderland's subsequent relegation as Newcastle bounced back. The North-East therefore awaits the resumption of a fixture which matters more than anything in the football crazy North-East of England.

Newcastle had won their fourth league title in 1927. During the 1950s, Newcastle won the FA Cup three times by 1955. United were cup-holders when they came to Roker Park on Boxing Day 1955 and equalled their biggest ever derby victory, winning 6-1 as they had at home in 1920. On the night of their big home defeat, Sunderland signed centre-forward Bill Holden. He would debut 24 hours

THE OLD FIRM DERBY

Celtic vs Rangers

Sometime in the late 19th century, a commentator is said to have explained the co-existence of Scottish football's 'big two' - Celtic and Rangers – as being "like two old, firm friends". While that joint descriptor is thought to be one of the reasons the term 'The Old Firm' is used for the two clubs today, the suggestion of a long, established friendship certainly hasn't prevailed over the decades.

Rangers are the fourth oldest professional club in Scotland, formed in March 1872 by four rowing enthusiasts: brothers Moses and Peter McNeil, Peter Campbell and William McBeath. 'The Gers' played early 'home' matches at Glasgow Green's Fleshers Haugh in the city's East End, before a move west to Burnbank Park in 1875 and then, the world-renowned Ibrox Stadium, to the south of the River Clyde in 1889. While Rangers moved around Glasgow in their early history, Celtic have always remained in the East End.

Celtic were formed at a meeting in St. Mary's Church on East Rose Street (now Forbes Street) in Calton on the 6th of November 1887 and played at the 'original' Celtic Park in Parkhead -

around 500 meters from the current ground – between 1888 and 1892. As fate would have it, Celtic's inaugural fixture at the venue was a 5-2 victory over Rangers on the 28th of May 1888.

By the time the two sides met in the Scottish Cup Final 16 years later, Celtic and Rangers had become two of the country's biggest clubs, with 16 major trophies – including nine top flight titles - between them. It was ahead of the 1904 final that the first-known reference to the term, the 'Old Firm' appeared in print, with a satirical cartoon in a football periodical - 'The Scottish Referee' - depicting an elderly man with a sandwich board reading "Patronise The Old Firm: Rangers, Celtic Ltd". This was a dig at a perception at the time that the two teams were working together to maximise their commercial advantage.

This perception was a contributing factor in mass disorder when the two sides met for another Scottish Cup Final in 1909. The original match finished in a 2-2 draw, prompting a replay seven days later. With the score level at 1-1 after 90 minutes of the replay, the crowd assumed extra-time would follow. However, competition rules stated extra-time would only be held

if the scores were level after a second replay. When it became clear extra-time would not be played, false rumour spread around Hampden Park that the result of the final was being manipulated to increase ticketing revenue. The crowd invaded the pitch, tore down the goalposts and even attacked mounted police and the fire brigade, with over 100 injuries reported as a result. A second replay was not scheduled by the Scottish Football Association, which meant the trophy was not presented that year. While there were no reports of conflict between the two sets of fans at that final, a footballing rivalry between the sides was very much alive in the early 20th century.

The collapse of a wooden stand at Ibrox in April 1902 led to Rangers having to rebuild their home ground for a second time, after an expensive expansion project only years earlier. Faced with financial difficulties, the club had to sell their best players. Celtic capitalised on Rangers' weakness, winning six consecutive titles between 1905 and 1910, much to the displeasure of the blue half of Glasgow. It was around this time that resentment between the supporter bases started to become far deeper rooted than football alone.

"A complicated battle on and off the pitch, intertwined with various political and religious undertones, the Glasgow showdown between Rangers and Celtic is quite possibly the most heated football rivalry in the world"

– Bleacher Report

Celtic's formation back in 1887 came on the promise the club would deliver finances and resources to a poverty-stricken Irish Catholic community in Glasgow's East End – many of whom had emigrated from Ireland to Scotland as a result of the Great Famine (1845-1852). While few records exist of Celtic's income reaching those causes, the football club quickly became a beacon of hope for the local population who had experienced marginalisation in areas of Glasgow society.

From the fifth century, Scotland had been a Roman Catholic country. After the Scottish Reformation of 1560, the Scottish Parliament renounced the Pope's authority and adopted Presbyterianism (the Church of Scotland) as its state religion. The influx of Irish Catholic immigrants in Glasgow from around the mid-19th century onwards increased competition for employment and housing in the city. "This sometimes led to antagonism and conflict between competing groups of workers over housing and jobs," explains anti-sectarianism organisation 'Nil By Mouth'. "Widespread discrimination in entering employment, and certain established social networks, also fuelled tensions between the Catholic and Protestant communities in Scotland."

While Celtic's origins are firmly embedded in Irish Catholicism, Rangers appeared not to have any particular religious leaning in their early history, although former Gers vice-chairman Matt Taylor claimed back in 1967; "We (Rangers) were formed in 1873 as a Protestant boys club". The club's links to Presbyterianism appear to have begun in the 1910s, when Belfast firm Harland and Wolff opened a shipyard in Govan, just a short walk from Rangers' Ibrox ground. Harland and Wolff's Belfast workforce at the time was overwhelmingly Protestant and this was reflected in the influx of workers to the Glasgow yard from Northern Ireland who were almost exclusively Presbyterian. The many hundreds of Ulster Protestants who made the move

across the Irish Sea adopted their new local club, Rangers, as their team.

Links between Rangers and Presbyterianism were enhanced in 1914 when the club hosted a fundraising benefit match against Partick Thistle for the Grand Orange Lodge in Glasgow. Ties between Rangers and the Orange Order – an organisation founded by Ulster Protestants in County Armagh in 1795 during a period of Protestant-Catholic conflict – increased after World War I when directors and players attended their functions. Between the 1930s and 1970s, there was an unwritten rule at Ibrox that the club would not employ any player or staff member who was openly Catholic.

In addition to a clear religious divide existing between Celtic and Rangers, author Richard Wilson points to a "series of complex disputes" in his book 'Inside the Divide' that have served to further polarise the clubs and their supporters. This includes notions of Northern Ireland-related politics, national identity and social ideology. Throughout much of the 20th century, Rangers fans tended to be 'native' Scots and Ulster Scots while Celtic were usually Irish-Scots. Gers followers were predominantly loyalist and conservative in their political and social ideology while Celtic fans tended to support socialism and the movement for a united Ireland. Such division was – and to a lesser extent, still is – the basis for such a hostile rivalry between Celtic and Rangers today.

The rivalry has also grown as a result of the unparalleled success of the clubs, meaning they are almost always in direct competition for the country's biggest prizes. As of April 2022, the Old Firm have won 106 Scottish League championships since 1890 - 85% of top-flight Scottish titles on offer between then and now. Rangers have won 55 titles to Celtic's 51 while the two clubs have claimed 73 Scottish Cups (Celtic with 40 and Rangers with 33) and 47 Scottish League Cups (Rangers with 27 and Celtic with 20) between them. Both

have experienced glory on the European stage too, with Celtic becoming the first British team to win the European Cup in 1967 while Rangers won the European Cup Winners' Cup in 1972.

Both Celtic and Rangers were the only clubs to have played in every top flight season of Scottish football up until 2012 when Rangers entered financial difficulties. The club, trading as 'The Rangers Football Club PLC' was liquidated that year, with administrators eventually selling the business and assets of Rangers to a new company 'The Rangers Football Club Ltd', operated by Charles Green. Other member clubs of the Scottish Premier League refused to allow the new company to adopt the same league membership as the old company, but Rangers did at least gain membership of the Scottish Football League. The club were admitted to the Scottish Third Division in 2012/13, winning the fourth tier title that season followed by the third tier in 2013/14 and the second tier in 2015/16.

In Rangers' absence from the top-flight, Celtic were able to continue a period of domination – winning nine titles in a row between 2012 and 2020. It was the Gers who finally broke this run, winning the Scottish Premiership title in 2020/21 under the management of Steven Gerrard. Prior to this, both clubs had previously achieved nine-in-a-row championships. Celtic managed the feat between 1966 and 1974 while Rangers did it between 1989 and 1997. Other than Rangers' aforementioned absence from the top flight, rarely has the Old Firm's collective dominance of Scottish football been threatened. Since 1986, one half of the Old Firm has won the Scottish League every season and in all but one of seventeen seasons between 1995/96 and 2011/12, the clubs finished in the top two places.

The Old Firm's superiority also extends to cup competitions, with over half of all Scottish Cups having been won by either Rangers or Celtic, while 62% of all Scottish League Cups have ended up on either the blue or green side of Glasgow. There have been 29 Old Firm cup finals over the two competitions, the most recent of which was a 1-0 victory for the Hoops in the 2019 Scottish League Cup Final.

The Scottish League Cup Final of 1965 and both the 1969 and 1977 Scottish Cup Finals, which involved the Old Firm, saw scenes of unrest but nothing that compared to the 1980 Scottish Cup Final. After Celtic's 1-0 extra-time win at Hampden Park, rival fans invaded the pitch. Match commentator Archie MacPherson described the subsequent disorder – that saw fans fighting, throwing bricks and bottles and using wooden staves from terracing frames as weapons – "like a scene out of Apocalypse Now". Over 200 arrests were made and the sale of alcohol at sporting events in Scotland was prohibited from that day on.

There were more controversial scenes as Rangers hosted Celtic in a Scottish Premier Division fixture on the 17th of October 1987. An altercation after 17 minutes of the match saw Gers goalkeeper Chris Wood and Celtic's Frank McAvennie sent off. Outfield player Graham Roberts had to go in goal for Rangers for the rest of the 2-2 draw. Rangers' Terry Butcher, who had been booked for his involvement in the earlier scuffle between McAvennie and Woods, was shown a second yellow in the second half for an alleged coming together with Hoops goalkeeper Allen McKnight, although video replays showed there had been no contact. After Rangers' unlikely comeback from two goals down to force a 2-2 draw late on, Roberts was accused of waving to Rangers fans as if he were 'conducting' their singing, which included sectarian chanting. This was not proven in a court of law, but both Butcher and Woods were later charged with a breach of the peace and ordered to pay fines. Sixty arrests were made around the match which has become known as the 'Shame Game'.

There were disturbances too on the 2nd of May 1999 as Rangers won 3-0 at Celtic Park to secure the Scottish Premier League title. Shortly after sending off Celtic's Stéphane Mahé, referee Hugh Dallas was struck by a coin thrown from the home end, leaving him with a head wound which needed four stitches. Rangers' Rod Wallace and Celtic's Vidar Riseth were also sent off during a volatile match that saw fans run onto the pitch on more than one occasion; over 100 arrests were made. Once again, the term

'Shame Game' was used in the media to describe this particular fixture.

Sectarianism has blighted Old Firm matches over the decades too. Both clubs have set up campaigns such as Celtic's 'Bhoys Against Bigotry' and Rangers' 'Follow With Pride', as well as the cross-club 'Sense Over Sectarianism', in the attempt to educate and challenge attitudes and values. At the same time, the clubs are also keen to stress that football-related bigotry is part of a wider problem in Scotland.

"There's a thing in a football ground called a 90-minute bigot: someone who has got a friend of an opposite religion next door to them," explained then-Rangers Head of Safety Lawrence Macintyre, at a summit on the topic of sectarianism at Glasgow University in 2005. "But for that 90 minutes they shout foul religious abuse at each other and we've got to handle in the first instance the 90-minute bigot. If we can get [to] the person that doesn't mean it then we'll isolate the real racists and real bigots in numbers that are manageable to deal with."

Overtly sectarian songs such as 'Billy Boys', the 'Famine Song' and the 'Glasgow Celtic IRA' were outlawed in 2011 at a time when such religious bigotry was on the continual decline in Scotland. That same year though, it was reported that death threats, including a package containing a bullet had been sent to then-Celtic manager Neil Lennon – a Roman Catholic from Northern Ireland. Three years earlier it was reported two 'viable' parcel bombs had been sent to the former Celtic player and manager, leading Dr John Kelly of the University of Edinburgh to surmise that; "recent events have buried the myth that anti-Irish Catholic bigotry no longer exists."

A significant first step in diminishing religious bigotry in relation to the Old Firm – although it might not have felt like it until years later - came in 1989 when Rangers signed an openly Catholic player, Mo Johnston, who arrived from Celtic. There was a mixed initial reaction

to this acquisition on the blue side of Glasgow, with some Rangers fans burning their season tickets as old prejudices came to the surface once more. Others welcomed the opportunity to sign a top player from their big rivals and some lapsed fans, who had been troubled by religious discrimination, returned to Ibrox on the back of Johnston's signing. Celtic fans were furious with Johnston and dubbed him 'Judas' for previously agreeing, what was tantamount to, a pre-contract agreement at Celtic Park only to then move to Rangers. In the midst of this controversial transfer, little credit was given to Rangers' manager at the time, Graham Souness, for his part in attempting to end anti-Catholic discrimination at Ibrox. But it appeared to set a welcome precedence as further Catholic players signed for the Gers thereafter, including Lorenzo Amoruso, who became the first Catholic captain of Rangers nine years later.

In the 21st century, the various dividing lines between the Old Firm have become far more blurred, not least due to the decline in religiosity in Scotland. In 2017, the Scottish Attitudes Survey reported 58% of respondents said they 'had no religion at all' in comparison to a figure of 40% in 1999. Among major denominations, the Church of Scotland had seen a sharp decline in popularity, with just 18% saying they belong to the Kirk in 2017 compared to 35% at the turn of the century. This national trend is reflected in Glasgow where, increasingly, religious and political views and affiliations don't always go hand in hand with those traditionally associated with the football club they support.

A line from a Wikipedia entry on the Old Firm rivalry surmises; "In 21st century Glasgow: religious adherence, in general, is falling, marriages between Protestants and Catholics have never been higher and the old certainties – the Rangers supporter voting Conservative and the Celtic supporter voting Labour — are no longer in evidence."

While there is no love lost between Celtic and Rangers supporters, a move towards a rivalry that is based more on football and less on religion and/or politics can only be a good thing. "You still have Celtic and Rangers fans who hate each other, [but] perhaps more now just for being Celtic or Rangers fans, than necessarily Catholic or Protestant," Celtic fan Peter Joyce told Al Jazeera in a feature on the Old Firm derby in 2018, adding "As religion [in Scotland] has changed, so have the football teams."

EUROPE

When it comes to global television audiences, revenue and power, no continent on earth can match Europe's football leagues and specifically its 'Big Five' divisions: the Premier League in England, La Liga in Spain, the Bundesliga in Germany, Serie A in Italy and Ligue 1 in France.

The Premier League's latest international broadcast contract is worth a staggering £5.3bn over a three-year period, taking the value of its overall commercial partnerships between 2022 and 2025 to £10.5bn.

While England's top division stands head and shoulders above the rest in terms of its viewing figures and worth, Europe's other big leagues boast some pretty impressive statistics of their

own. In the last full season before COVID-19 struck - forcing matches all around the world to be played behind closed doors – the Bundesliga had the highest average attendance of any football league in the world. An average crowd of 43,458 passed through the turnstiles of Germany's 18 top flight clubs in 2018/19.

The Bundesliga's showpiece fixture is played between Bayern Munich and Borussia Dortmund. While 'Der Klassiker' lacks the history of more traditional German rivalries – such as Dortmund's 'Revierderby' with FC Schalke 04 and Bayern's Bavarian derby with 1. FC Nürnberg – the fact the two clubs have collected 18 of 21 Bundesliga titles on offer in the 21st century is an obvious reason why meetings between the pair take on such huge significance. Düsseldorf-based football fans Emma Storey and Marius Kortholt report on both 'Der Klassiker' and the 'Revierderby' for this book.

La Liga is home to two of the world's top four wealthiest clubs by revenue - with Real Madrid second in the latest of Deloitte Sports Business Group's Football Money League with a turnover of €644.9m in 2020/21 while FC Barcelona were fourth with €582.1m. The previous campaign had seen Barça top the list, with Real Madrid second, before the full impact of COVID-19 was felt.

Not only are Real and Barça Spain's wealthiest clubs, they are the teams who command most attention nationally and internationally. Barcelona's 4-0 win at the Santiago Bernabéu in March 2022 was watched by an audience in excess of 650 million across 180+ countries. La Liga as a whole had 2.5 billion viewers during the 2020/21 season.

Given their prominence in La Liga alone - with the two sides having won the most and second-most Spanish titles respectively - it is no surprise that 'Los Blancos' and the 'Blaugrana' have a huge rivalry.

Every major European country has its answer to El Clásico or Der Klassiker and France's is 'Le Classique'. Also known as 'Le Derby de France', the fixture features Olympique de Marseille and Paris Saint-Germain. As with the other clubs mentioned, Marseille and PSG are their country's two most successful clubs.

While this derby was originally dominated by 'Les Olympiens', the 2011 takeover at PSG by Qatar Sports Investments (QSI) transformed 'Les Parisiens' into one of the richest clubs in the world.

Italy's grand offering is Derby d'Italia – Inter Milan versus Juventus. Their

battle to be the country's top dog has seen a fierce rivalry develop between these past European Cup winners. As we will discover in this book, the 'Calciopoli' scandal of 2006 exacerbated the ill-feeling between the two clubs. Italy's biggest domestic rivalry is most definitely box office - over 650 million television viewers around the world tuned into a derby game between the pair in January 2021.

While the derby matches of the most successful clubs across Europe naturally attract the most global attention, there are rivalries across the continent every bit as fiery and hard-fought. COPA90's Eli Mengem has witnessed some incredible matches for his Derby Days series including the 'Derby della Capitale', between Rome's Lazio and Roma and El Derbi Madrileño that sees Atlético Madrid lock horns with city rivals Real Madrid.

Eli has also ventured beyond the 'Big Five' leagues where, arguably, certain rivalries have even greater cultural significance and hostility. He describes himself as being lucky to "still be alive to tell the tale"of the 'Eternal derby' that pits FK Partizan and Crvena zvezda in the Serbian capital, Belgrade, while he summed up the Budapest derby between Ferencvárosi TC and Újpest FC as "intense". The Sarajevo derby meanwhile, featuring FK Željezničar Sarajevo and FK Sarajevo, was – in Eli's words - "surprising" and "what experiencing derbies is all about".

From the very edge of Europe, Eli recalls his experiences of the 'Intercontinental Derby' for Football's Greatest Club Rivalries. This particular derby between Fenerbahçe SK and Galatasaray SK, in Istanbul, Turkey is so-called because one of its clubs are based on the European side of the city, the other on the Asian side. This meeting in April 2014 saw away fans banned due to past violence while on the pitch, there were 14 yellow cards and two reds.

EL CLÁSICO

Barcelona vs Real Madrid

FC Barcelona's motto describes the Blaugrana (Blue and Red) as 'Mes Que Un Club', meaning 'More Than A Club'. And in their long-standing rivalry with Real Madrid, there is a deep rooted and fundamental dislike of Los Blancos (The Whites), and vice-versa, that makes matches between the clubs 'more than a derby'.

Barcelona and Real Madrid - whose own motto is 'Hala Madrid y nada más' (Go Madrid and nothing more) – are two behemoths of not just Spanish but world football. Whatever way you look to measure the clubs – be it on trophies won, size of their stadia, number of fans, annual revenue or value – the La Liga giants are likely to be found at the top of the pile.

Barcelona were formed in 1899 by a group of English, German, Spanish and Swiss footballers led by Joan Gamper, who had also founded Swiss side FC Zürich a few years earlier. From their early history, FC Barcelona have been an important symbol for Catalan identity and an institution that was at odds with the dictatorships of Miguel Primo de Rivera and Francisco Franco during the 20th century. "The dictator (Miguel Primo de Rivera) considered his greatest enemies anyone who toyed with the idea of becoming more separate from Madrid, by pursuing their own devolved government and speaking their own language," wrote Jimmy Burns in his 1998 version of 'Barça: A People's Passion'. "Political Catalanism in all its manifestations came into his firing line, making a clash with FC Barcelona inevitable."

Real Madrid's origins go back to the foundation of Sociedad (originally named Sky Football) in 1897 by members of the Institución Libre de Enseñanza in Madrid, which included several Cambridge and Oxford University graduates. Conflict between members

eventually led to another club being set up called Nueva Sociedad de Football (New Society of Football), to distinguish themselves from Sky Football. This club was renamed 'Madrid Football Club' in 1901 and, after a new board presided by Juan Padrós had been elected, Madrid FC were officially founded. Madrid were renamed 'Real Madrid' in 1920 after King Alfonso XIII granted the title of 'Real', meaning 'Royal'.

After they were founded, both Barcelona and Real Madrid enjoyed early success. The Blaugrana lifted the Copa Macaya and participated in the first Copa de la Coronación (the forerunner of the Copa del Rey) Final in 1902 before winning the tournament's replacement in 1910. Meanwhile Madrid won four consecutive Copa del Rey between 1905 and 1908. Barcelona and Madrid met for the first time en route to Barça's appearance in

the 1902 Copa de la Coronación Final, as they triumphed 3-1 in the semi-finals.

Barcelona won the inaugural La Liga in 1929 while Real became champions of Spain in 1932 and 1933. These successes cemented both clubs' status as two of Spanish football's biggest and most popular clubs. Barcelona expanded their Les Cortes stadium from a capacity of 30,000 to 60,000 during the following decade while Real rebuilt the Estadio Real Madrid Club de Fútbol (now Santiago Bernabéu) and their training facilities, Ciudad Deportiva, during the 1940s.

This growth and success came amidst a volatile political back drop. When Miguel Primo de Rivera completed a Mussolini-inspired military coup on the 13th of September 1923, he closed down the Catalan government and banned the use of the Catalan language. He angered the Catalan people further when he forbid any tribute to Orfeó Català – a choral society set up in 1891 by local composers Lluís Millet Pages and Amadeu Vives – prior to a fundraising match for the organisation at Les Cortes on the 14th of June 1925.

The match between Barcelona and Jupiter went ahead irrespectively. As Jimmy Burns notes in Barça: A People's Passion, "The mood of defiance was signalled by the presence in the executive box, alongside the Barça directors, of two prominent Catalanist politicians, Francesc Cambó and Joaquin Ventosa Calvell, together with the founder of the Orfeó, Lluís Millet Pages." At half time in that particular match, a band of the British Royal Marines started to play the Spanish national anthem but the song was drowned out by boos and whistles from supporters. The band

started playing the British national anthem instead which was cheered.

The incident saw FC Barcelona issued with a military edict, which saw Les Cortes closed for six months while Gamper was forced to relinquish his presidency of the club. "The 1920s with its recurring pattern of repression and reaction – closures, censorship,

strikes, demonstrations – inevitably politicised life inside and outside the stadium," explains Burns.

Catalonia suffered further repression during and after the Spanish Civil War of 1936 to 1939, which halted top-flight league football in Spain. In 1936 Barça president Josep Sunyol, who was a member of the 'Republican Left of Catalonia', was arrested and executed without trial by the troops of Nationalist Francisco Franco. During the war, Franco led a coup d'état against the democratic

Second Spanish Republic and eventually ruled Spain between 1939 and 1975.

Despite the fact that Real Madrid suffered during the war – with president Rafael Sánchez Guerra captured by Franco supporters – and that some Barcelona directors had a good relationship with Franco, the Francoist regime created a polarised view of the two clubs.

"The simplistic view is of Barcelona and Real Madrid representing left and right on the political spectrum, of Real Madrid

while Barcelona were the team of the resistance. The connection to Franco also spawned the on-going idea of Real Madrid being a right-wing club and Barcelona being a leftist organisation.

Real Madrid were the most successful team of the Francoist era, with 14 La Liga titles, six Copa del Generalísimo (now Copa Del Rey) and six European Cups. Barcelona won eight titles and six Copa del Generalísimo during this time. Despite Barça's relative success, there are some who believe Real Madrid's alignment with Franco prevented greater glory during that period. An infamous, two-legged Copa del Generalísimo semi-final of 1943 has served such conspiracy theories.

Barça triumphed 3-0 in the first leg of the tie at Les Corts – a match in which Real complained to referee Fombona Fernández about the legitimacy of all three goals. Commenting in an interview about the pretext of the second leg, former Barça player Josep Valle recalled; "The DND and ABC newspaper wrote all sorts of scurrilous lies, really terrible things, winding up the Madrid fans like never before." Real were two goals up within half an hour of the second leg at the Chamartín (Real Madrid's then-home ground) and went on to win 11-1. It has been alleged, although never proven, that the Barça players were pressured into losing the game by supporters of Francoist Spain. Then-Barcelona president Enrique Piñeyro Queralt complained to the Royal Spanish Football Federation about circumstances surrounding the match and subsequently resigned from his position in August 1943, criticising "a campaign that the press has run against Barcelona for a week and which culminated in the shameful day at Chamartín". "This was the game that first formed the identification of Madrid as the team of the dictatorship and Barcelona as its victims," wrote Lowe in Fear and Loathing in La Liga: Barcelona Vs Real Madrid.

Real Madrid completed the signing of one of the greatest players in their history in 1953 with the capture of

being Franco's team and Barcelona's being the democrats, the freedom fighters," Sid Lowe, author of 'Fear and Loathing in La Liga: Barcelona Vs Real Madrid', told Eli Mengem in COPA90's Derby Days feature on El Clásico.

With perceived strong links between Real Madrid and Franco during his 36-year reign ('perceived' being the operative word as we will discover in this chapter), a general view in Catalonia during the time was that Los Blancos had become the club of the regime

the club's all-time record goalscorer (a record surpassed by Raúl in 2009 and again later by Cristiano Ronaldo).

In 1970, a Copa del Generalísimo tie served to intensify the narrative of Barcelona being the 'victims' of 'Franco's Madrid'. The first leg of the quarter final, staged in Madrid – with Real's home named after legendary former player and president Santiago Bernabéu by this stage – saw Los Blancos record a 2-0 win. A crowd of nearly 100,000 packed into the Nou Camp – Barça's home from 1957 to date – for the second leg. Carles 'Charly' Rexach gave the Blaugrana an early first half lead but Real Madrid responded with an equaliser from the penalty spot, after Basque referee Emilio Guruceta penalised Joaquim Rifé's challenge on Manolo Velázquez.

Guruceta's awarding of the spot-kick – converted by Real Madrid's Amancio – was a dubious decision to say the least. Velázquez appeared to be outside the Barcelona penalty area when Rifé's tackle came in, with the referee some 30-yards away from the incident. In the ensuing chaos, Barcelona's Eladio was sent-off shortly after for mocking the referee. Howls of derision rang out from home supporters as a result of these decisions while some Barcelona players briefly walked off the pitch in protest, only to be persuaded to return by then-manager Vic Buckingham.

"Towards the end of that game, there was a spontaneous eruption amongst the spectators and thousands of seat cushions were thrown prior to there being a pitch invasion," commented Burns in a 2018 Tottenham Hotspur-Barcelona programme article. "The so-called 'Guruceta case' became a defining moment in the history not only of El Clásico but of modern Catalonia. It was almost like a revolution breaking out."

The Di Stéfano transfer and the 'Guruceta case' are still cited to this day as means of 'proving' the 'favour' Real Madrid gained during the Francoist era. "There is no shortage of people who would claim

Argentinian striker Alfredo Di Stéfano. The transfer was a complicated affair. Amidst a players' strike in Argentina, during which time Di Stéfano turned out for Colombian side Club Millonarios, both Los Blancos and Barcelona claimed to have secured his registration. After intervention from FIFA, it was decided the clubs should 'share' the player, with the Argentine set to feature for Madrid in 1953/54 and 1955/56 and Barca in 1954/55 and 1956/57. The messy situation eventually led to Enric Martí Carreto stepping down as Barcelona president and, a few weeks later, Barça's board withdrawing its claim to Di Stéfano, allowing Real Madrid to sign him on a permanent basis. The player went on to score 307 goals for Los Blancos between 1953 and 1964, becoming

that Los Blancos' success and wealth during that period was in some way owed to their underhand connections with the Generalísimo," wrote Nick Fitzgerald in a feature for These Football Times in 2017.

"There are various reasons that have led to this becoming an established discourse, and the role of Barcelona in perpetuating the myth should not be underestimated. The story of Real Madrid's connections to Franco fits with Barcelona's preferred narrative, which likes to see the club as symbolising the established order and the conservative, centralised Spain whereas they themselves symbolise democracy and an independent Catalonia – the plucky underdogs, who succeeded in spite of intense persecution from the regime."

Lowe agreed with Fitzgerald's take on the 'discourse' surrounding Barcelona-Real Madrid when he spoke to COPA90: "The former president [of] Real Madrid, a guy called Ramón Mendoza, once described the Clasico as 'a story that's a myth but that suits us both'. And that's the bottom line. He saw this as a power struggle in which both teams… it suited them to lie. It suited them to embrace this idea. Why? Because it helped them

to create a narrative, to create a story that eclipsed the rest of Spain and put these two at the very head of everything."

While there is no doubt the region of Catalonia and its people suffered under the rule of Franco, the suggestion that FC Barcelona were treated unfairly during this era is far more debatable. So too is the suggestion Real Madrid were afforded an unfair advantage as a result of their relationship with the dictator.

"Franco did to some extent align himself with the club – but it would be a huge step to suggest that their success is in some way owed to this connection," wrote Fitzgerald. "The common assumption is that Real Madrid were great because Franco supported them, but it would be more accurate to say that Franco supported them because they were great."

Irrespective of whether the rivalry between Barcelona and Real Madrid has been built on fact, fiction or a mixture of both, El Clásico is quite possibly the biggest derby fixture in European football. Political positioning and the notions of Spanish and Catalan nationalism are undoubted subplots in this rivalry but perhaps more saliently, is the fact that Barcelona and Real Madrid are Spain's largest and most successful clubs – arguably, Europe's too.

As with Boca Juniors and River Plate in Argentina, the two clubs have differing footballing ideals. Real Madrid, known for their multi-million 'Galácticos' (Spanish for galactics, referring to superstars) are expected by their fans to win at any costs. This philosophy has been taken quite literally over the years. Cristiano Ronaldo was signed by Los Blancos for a fee of around €100m in 2009 while Gareth Bale arrived from Tottenham Hotspur a few years later for a similar fee. Back in 2000 meanwhile, Los Blancos completed the then-world record signing of Barcelona's Luis Figo for €62m. The disdain the Blaugrana felt for their star for what they viewed as defection was demonstrated when they threw a pig's head – amongst other things – at their former star during a derby match at the Nou Camp in November 2002.

Real Madrid have lived up to their fans' 'win at all costs' expectation with 34 La Liga titles, 13 European Cups, three Intercontinental Cups and four FIFA Club World Cups won to date – all records.

In keeping with the 'Mes Que Un Club' motto, first uttered by former Barcelona president Narcís de Carreras in 1968, the club website reads, "We are more than a team of great stars, we are more than a stadium full of dreams, we are more than the goals we've scored and more than the trophies that we've won throughout our history". Barça have immense pride in being a member-led outfit with "principles as humility, effort, ambition, teamwork and respect just as important as the achievement of sporting success". Blaugrana draw particular satisfaction from the development of players through their renowned La Masia youth academy and in 2010, three products of that - Lionel Messi, Andrés Iniesta and Xavi - were chosen as the three best players in the world in the FIFA Ballon d'Or awards.

"For a player, El Clasico, is the most beautiful match that exists in football"

- Zinedine Zidane

THE DERBY D'ITALIA

Inter Milan vs Juventus

Juventus' popularity across Italy is reflected in one of the club's many nicknames: Il Fidanzata D'Italia, meaning 'the Girlfriend of Italy'. Research conducted by Demos & Pi and published in September 2016 stated over 12 million Italians – roughly 34% of the nation's football fans – follow Juve, making them the best-supported club in Italy. La Vecchia Signora (the Old Lady) are also by far and away Italy's most successful team, having won 70 major trophies as of March 2022.

As Juventus tops polls for being Italy's most followed team, they are also the side most non-Bianconeri (Black and Whites) supporting Italians love to hate. In a September 2015 survey, conducted by Coop and the Osservatorio Capitale Sociale, 43% of respondents said La Vecchia Signora were their 'least favourite team' with Inter Milan second on 24%.

Supporters of Inter, whose club have won the second most Scudetto (19) after Juve (36), have particular cause to dislike the Turin outfit as a result of a controversial ending to the 1960/61 Serie A season. Inter won 3-1 at the San Siro in the first meeting of the clubs that season on the 18th of December 1960. The reverse fixture on the 16th of April 1961 was suspended by match referee Carlo Gambarotta after 31 minutes as supporters invaded the pitch at Juventus' former Stadio Comunale Vittorio Pozzo ground, with the score goalless at the time.

A meeting of the Federazione Italiana Giuoco Calcio (FIGC) on the 24th of April 1961 awarded a 2-0 win to Inter as a result of the postponement, which put the Nerazzurri (Black and Blues) firmly on course to win an eighth Serie A title. Juventus' 1-0 away defeat at Padova on the 30th of May 1961, coupled with Inter's 3-0 triumph, meant the Biscione (Big Grass Snake) captain Armando Picchi had one hand on the Scudetto. But Inter were rocked by Juventus' decision to appeal the awarding of the 2-0 win to the Nerazzurri in lieu of the April postponement to the Federal Justice Court on the 3rd of June 1961 – the day before the final round of Serie A fixtures. The FIGC – then headed by Bianconeri president Umberto Agnelli – ordered the game be replayed on the 10th of June 1961. This move was seen by Inter as effectively handing the title to Juventus and Nerazzurri president Angelo Moratti and coach Helenio Herrera took the decision to field a youth team in the rearranged

match. Juve won 9-1, collected their 12th title and so a bitter rivalry was born.

Football in Italy during the 1960s was dominated by the two clubs' battle for power. Inter got revenge for the 1960/61 season with a title success of their own in 1962/63, as they finished four points clear of second-placed Juventus. The Nerazzurri won the Scudetto again in 1964/65 but were denied a domestic 'double' when Giampaolo Menichelli gave Juve a 1-0 win over Inter in the Coppa Italia Final of August 1965. Juventus had become just the second team in Italian history to win the double back in 1959/60 after city rivals Torino achieved it in 1942/43.

The Nerazzurri completed a unique 'double' of their own in 1964/65 though as they retained their European Cup crown. Inter beat Real Madrid 3-1 in the 1964 final and followed that up with a 1-0 win over Benfica in 1965. They also won the Intercontinental Cup in those respective years, enhancing their reputation as one of club football's greatest-ever teams. A third Serie A title in four years followed in 1965/66.

Inter and Juventus went toe-to-toe for the Serie A title in 1966/67. Going into the final round of league fixtures on the 1st of June 1967, Inter needed just a draw in their away match at Mantova or for Juve to fail to win at home to Lazio to become Serie A winners once again. Alas, a goal from former Nerazzurri forward Beniamino Di Giacomo gave Mantova a 1-0 win while a 2-1 win for the Bianconeri saw Juventus take the title in unlikely circumstances. The drama of the 1966/67 season had Italian football fans gripped and it was during this campaign that journalist and former La Gazzetta dello Sport editor-in-chief Gianni Brera coined the term 'Derby d'Italia' to sum-up the national significance of head-to-head meetings and the overall rivalry between Inter Milan and Juventus.

Inter were Serie A winners in 1970/71 but the decade belonged to Juventus, who claimed the Scudetto in 1971/72, 1972/73, 1974/75, 1976/77 and 1977/78. There was also European glory for La Vecchia Signora in the shape of the UEFA Cup in 1977. For their part, Il Biscione won the Coppa Italia in 1978 and claimed the Scudetto in 1979/80. The Nerazzurri saw their achievements of the 1980s overshadowed by Juventus too. The Bianconeri won the title in 1980/81, 1981/82, 1983/84 and 1985/86 and collected the European Cup Winners' Cup in 1984, while Inter were Coppa Italia winners in 1982 and champions of Italy in 1988/89.

Juventus landed the biggest continental prize of all during the decade, lifting the European Cup for the first time in

1985. Their success – which saw them become the first club to have won all three major European trophies (European Cup, UEFA Cup and the European Cup Winners' Cup) – was marred by rioting prior to the final against Liverpool at Heysel Stadium in Brussels that resulted in the tragic death of 39 supporters.

Sadly, elements of Inter's support have used the Heysel disaster as a means of provoking Juventus fans. During a 2011 clash between the two sides at the San Siro, a banner was unfurled in the home end that read "Acciaio scadente: nostalgia dell'Heysel", which roughly translates as "poor quality iron - nostalgia for Heysel". This banner was used in the context of the newly-built Juventus Stadium and the fatal collapse of a wall at Heysel prior to the start of the 1985 European Cup Final. The response from some Juventus fans during the 29th of October 2011 match was in equally poor taste with Goal.com reporting that Bianconeri sang; "offensive chants mocking the death of former Inter president Giacinto Facchetti and insulting current supremo Massimo Moratti, as well as former Nerazzurri director and FIGC commissioner Guido Rossi".

Inter Milan enjoyed European success during the 1990s with three UEFA Cups collected in 1991, 1994 and 1998. The decade proved a difficult one for them on the domestic front though. Not only did Juventus win three Serie A titles and the UEFA Champions League in the same timeframe, they saw city rivals AC Milan enjoy a golden period with five Scudetto and two European Cups. After winning Serie A in 1989, it wasn't until 2006 that Inter claimed another title.

The 1997/98 season was a particularly painful one for Inter, despite a UEFA Cup win. They led the Serie A table up until a 1-0 home defeat to Bari on the 18th of January 1998 but remained hot on the heels of title rivals Juventus. In a head-to-head clash between the two sides at the Stadio delle Alpi on the 26th of April 1998, Juve led 1-0 through a 21st-minute strike from the legendary Alessandro Del Piero, when referee Piero Ceccarini waved

away claims from Inter for what seemed like a clear penalty following a challenge by Mark Iuliano on Ronaldo. Less than 60 seconds later, the Bianconeri were awarded a soft spot kick after Taribo West challenged Del Piero. Although Gianluca Pagliuca saved Del Piero's penalty, Inter were incensed by two perceived injustices. Substitute Zé Elias was sent off in the second half and the Milanese side were unable to prevent a 1-0 defeat to Juventus, who finished the season five points clear of their big rivals in second.

Inter fans were also crying foul in the summer of 2004 when future Italian World Cup-winning captain Fabio Cannavaro departed the San Siro to sign for Juventus. The defender became a figure of hate for elements of the Nerazzurri support as he completed a transfer every bit as controversial as Luis Figo's move from Barcelona to Real Madrid and Sol Campbell's departure from Tottenham Hotspur to Arsenal. The pain of Cannavaro's departure was heightened for Inter fans as the defender won back-to-back Scudetto with La Vecchia Signora in 2005 and 2006. Little did they know at the time that Cannavaro and Juventus would be stripped of those titles.

A match fixing scandal in Italy's top two leagues, which came to light in May 2006, proved to be a massive moment in the history of Italian football and the Inter Milan-Juventus rivalry. Of the five teams implicated in the 'Calciopoli' scandal, the actions of Juventus meant they were the most heavily punished. La Vecchia Signora were stripped of their 2004/05 Serie A title and were downgraded to the bottom spot in the division in 2005/06, securing their relegation to Serie B in the process. Their title from that campaign was reallocated to Inter Milan, ending the Biscione's 17-year wait to be champions of Italy once again. Key players such as Cannavaro, Lilian Thuram and Zlatan Ibrahimović all left Juventus as a result of their relegation.

Ibrahimović's departure was particularly tough for the Bianconeri as he signed

for Inter Milan – the club the Swede claimed to have supported as a child. In Ibrahimovic's first season at the San Siro, Inter won the Scudetto with a record 97 points. Juventus did at least secure promotion straight back to the top flight in 2006/07, winning Serie B. La Vecchia Signora were straight back in the hunt for the Serie A crown the following season, as they finished fourth, but rivals Inter took the title once again. Il Biscione's domination of Italian football continued with further Scudetto in 2008/09 and 2009/10. The latter campaign proved to be Inter's season of seasons. Under the management of José Mourinho, they also won the Coppa Italia and UEFA Champions League to complete the 'treble' becoming the first and, to date, only Italian club ever to do so.

Around the same time Inter celebrated their treble success, Juventus director Luciano Moggi stoked ill-feeling between La Vecchia Signora and Il Biscione by suggesting the late Giacinto Facchetti, who was Inter's president before his death in 2006, had been involved in corrupt activity. Moggi was eventually cleared of a slander charge brought against him by Facchetti's son Gianfelice.

After a period of domination by Inter Milan, the appointment of Antonio Conte as Juventus manager in 2011 tipped the balance of power firmly in the Bianconeri's favour. He won every Serie A title available to him (three) prior to being appointed as Italy manager in 2014. Massimiliano Allegri continued Juve's run of consecutive titles with triumphs in 2014/15, 2015/16, 2016/17, 2017/18 and 2018/19, as well as Coppa Italia successes in four of those five seasons. He also guided the club to Champions League Final appearances in 2015 and 2017.

Juventus' run of nine straight Serie A titles was finally broken in 2021 by arch-rivals Inter Milan, who were managed by ex-Juventus player and boss Antonio Conte during the campaign. The 2021/22 season once again saw both clubs involved in the Serie A title race as their fight for national superiority continued.

"The derby d'Italia
is a very difficult
match, five out of
five on the scale"

- Massimiliano Allegri

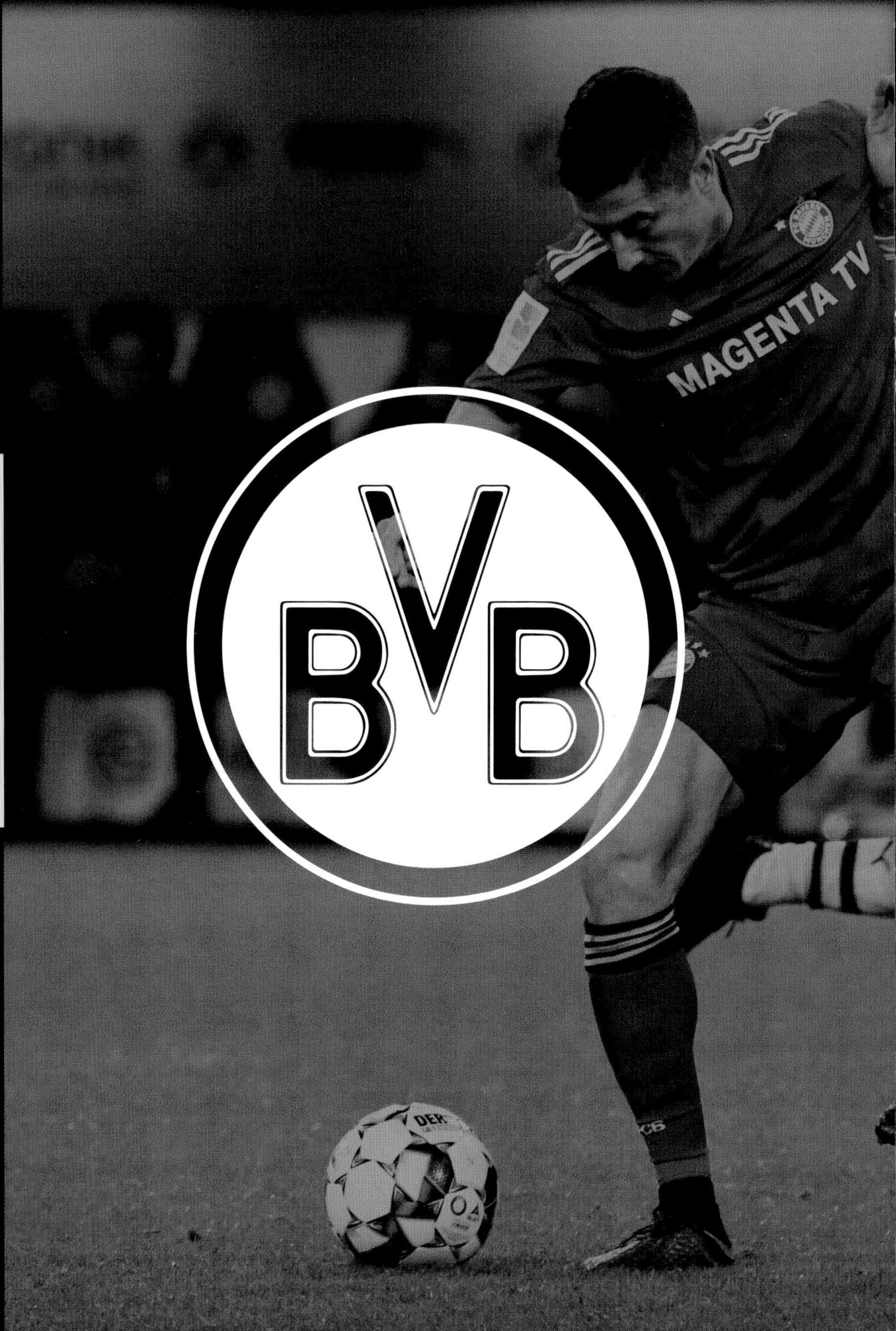
MAGENTA TV
BVB

DER KLASSIKER

Borussia Dortmund vs Bayern Munich
By Emma Storey and Marius Kortholt

The smell of bratwurst and beer drifts through the cold night air, as the stands rumble with the opening bars of "You'll Never Walk Alone" which thousands of fans are singing in unison. It's the Westfalenstadion on a dark Saturday night, and the air is crackling with tension ahead of the latest instalment of Der Klassiker; Borussia Dortmund vs. Bayern Munich. Although you're more likely to be met with a bemused shake of the head or scornful laugh if you call it that here.

"No-one calls it that. It's a name made up by television," explains Marius Kortholt, a born-and-bred lifelong Dortmund fan.

"Usually when someone comes up to me and says 'Ahhh, Der Klassiker!', I try not to roll my eyes. It's hard, because it's usually people from other countries, who started knowing the game this way, but it's not 'Der Klassiker', it's 'Dortmund-Bayern' for us; everyone knows what it is. It's about everything, it's about the crown in German football."

The name may be less than authentic, but there's nothing false about the passionate rivalry between the Bundesliga's two biggest clubs. "When it's Bayern, it's electrifying, it's so tense you can feel the heat of it coming," continues Kortholt, as we jostle for position on the world-famous Yellow Wall (die Gelbe Wand), the largest single-tier football terrace in Europe.

"You run through every scenario in your head: if you win, if you draw, how will the game go, what will the team be like, in every minute before kick-off. Even in the days before the game it starts building up, you can feel it, like lightning going through your body."

Standing on the Yellow Wall certainly feels like an electric shock of an experience; its throbbing intensity prompting goosebumps that have nothing to do with the freezing night. The Südtribüne (South Stand), as it is more conventionally known, is 328ft long and 131ft high, and holds almost 25,000 standing fans at capacity. It's an awe-inspiring sight when in full flow, driven at its heart by BVB's hardcore ultras, who lead the singing (and jumping!) through megaphones and beating drums that echo the length and breadth of the

stand, as the giant flags synonymous with German football wave gracefully in sync with the deafening sound.

This passionate support is credited with many a famous Klassiker victory. "If you are the enemy, it crushes you but if you have her at your back as a goalkeeper, it's a fantastic feeling," according to former Dortmund captain Roman Weidenfeller. And the effect on the opposition shouldn't be underestimated. When former Bayern Munich midfielder Bastian Schweinsteiger was asked before a game against BVB if it was the opposing players or their coach he was more wary of, he admitted, "It's the Yellow Wall I'm most afraid of". Compared to some of European football's other big rivalries, Bayern-Dortmund is relatively young, only really coming to fruition in the last thirty years or so, and

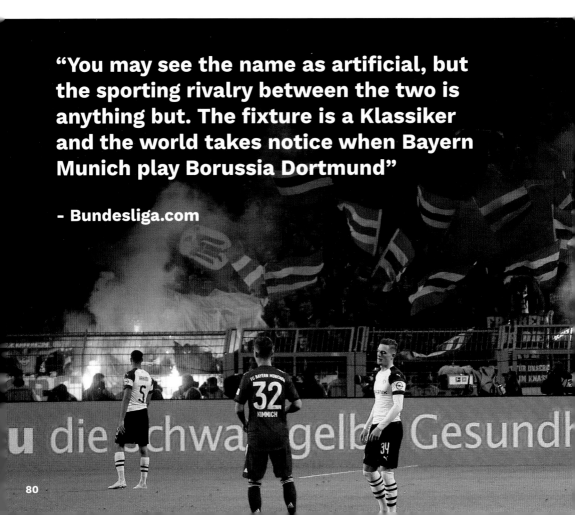

"You may see the name as artificial, but the sporting rivalry between the two is anything but. The fixture is a Klassiker and the world takes notice when Bayern Munich play Borussia Dortmund"

– Bundesliga.com

pre-dated by the original head-to-heads in Germany, such as Bayern against another Borussia (Mönchengladbach) and Dortmund's fiery Ruhr derby with Schalke. For much of the 1960s and 70s, BVB were a club constantly in flux, following a number of top four finishes in the Bundesliga with relegation to German football's second tier, where they languished for four consecutive seasons. In the meantime a dominant Bayern swept aside all challengers on their way to eleven Bundesliga titles and three consecutive European Cups.

Indeed, it's fair to say that a credible rivalry was the furthest thing from anyone's mind when Bayern, featuring the likes of Gerd Müller, Franz Beckenbauer and Uli Hoeness in the line-up, notched up a record 11-1 humiliation of Dortmund in the 1971/72 league season.

Fast forward 20 years though, and the story was beginning to change.

After 18 wins for Bayern and just 10 for Dortmund in 41 league meetings between the two, Dortmund hired Ottmar Hitzfeld as head coach in 1991. What followed was a revelation for the Ruhrpott side. In his first season, the Dortmunders beat the Bavarians 3-0 both home and away, helping to condemn Bayern to a 10th place-finish; their second-worst Bundesliga campaign. That was followed by BVB's long-awaited first Bundesliga title in 1994/95, finishing six points clear of Bayern in sixth.

The following season saw the first real title race between the two, with Dortmund again coming out on top, successfully defending their Bundesliga crown, and ending the season once again

six points clear of Bayern, who finished as runners-up. In 1996/97, the tables were turned, with Bayern reclaiming the title under Giovanni Trapattoni, as their rivals ended third. But it could be argued that Dortmund ended up having the last laugh. They went on to claim their first Champions League title in the same year, not only beating a star-studded Juventus side 3-1 on an unforgettable night, but doing it in Bayern's own home - the Olympiastadion in Munich - to well and truly steal the spotlight.

It was the Champions League that would again take centre stage the very next season, as the two met in the quarter-finals; the first time in the competition's history that two sides from the same country had faced each other. Dortmund prevailed thanks to a single goal from Stephane Chapuisat in the 19th minute of extra time, as the hard-fought rivalry got its first global audience.

When Hitzfeld crossed the Klassiker divide to take charge at Bayern in the summer of 1998, he took the balance of power with him. In six sparkling seasons in Munich, he won four Bundesliga titles, two German Cups and the Champions League, while for Dortmund it became a period of mid-table mediocrity.

After former BVB player Matthias Sammer was appointed as their coach in 2000, the signs looked more positive for Dortmund. They'd certainly got under Bayern's skin, as an explosive clash in April 2001 proved when it became known as the dirtiest match in Bundesliga history. Fourteen cards were dished out over the 90 minutes, including three reds. Bayern ended the match with nine men, the game in a 1-1 draw.

But just as the rivalry was approaching its boiling point, its very existence was almost extinguished. After years of financial mismanagement, BVB descended into the abyss in 2004. Forced to sell their ground and on the brink of bankruptcy, Dortmund were unable to even pay their players. In an unprecedented show of solidarity (certainly for football fans in other countries), Bayern came to their rivals' aid, loaning them €2m to cover salaries and ensure they finished the season. The money was repaid in full within a year, and how much of a decisive role it played in Dortmund's recovery as a German football powerhouse depends now on which side you speak to about it!

Bayern certainly used Dortmund's on-pitch struggles to their advantage though, dominating Der Klassiker throughout the noughties. The Bavarians beat BVB eleven times in the Bundesliga, as well as in the German Cup Final to complete their domestic double in 2007/08. But another Dortmund resurgence was just around the corner, propelled by a man who has become one of Europe's most successful and high-profile coaches: Jürgen Klopp.

With Klopp at the helm, and the likes of Mats Hummels, Robert Lewandowski and Mario Götze playing the now-famous "Gegenpressing" style of aggressive football, Dortmund stormed to consecutive Bundesliga titles in 2010/11 and 2011/12, securing the latter in a thrilling Der Klassiker at the Westfalenstadion. Lewandowski scored the only goal before Arjen Robben missed an 85th minute penalty, while the Yellow Wall played their own part in the victory by pelting Bayern goalkeeper Manuel Neuer with bananas throughout the match. That was the last of four consecutive league victories over Bayern, and BVB followed it up by spectacularly thrashing the Bavarians 5-2 in the 2012 German Cup Final to secure their first domestic double. For the first time in decades, it appeared that Bayern were no longer the best team in Germany.

"It meant the world basically. It was unthinkable," remembers Kortholt. "Not just that we'd won our first double ever, the only double we have ever won, but defeating Bayern every single game. It felt like we were at the top now and they could only look up at what we'd done. It's indescribable how that felt."

Bayern's response to this seemingly seismic shift was swift and emphatic. They deposed Dortmund as champions in both the Bundesliga and German Cup in 2012/13, setting the stage for the biggest showdown of them all, as the two teams travelled to London's iconic Wembley Stadium to contest the first all-German Champions League Final.

The match would go down as one of the best finals in European history, although it took an hour for the first goal to be scored. The pulsating atmosphere drove both teams on towards what looked like certain extra time, with the score deadlocked at 1-1 heading into the final minute of normal time. But Robben had other ideas, snatching a dramatic, late winner to spark jubilation in the red half of the stadium. Bayern were the first German side to complete the treble, cementing outgoing coach Jupp Heynckes' status as a Munich legend.

That night in Wembley would prove the end of an era for Dortmund. Not content with simply winning the treble, Bayern came after BVB's best players. Götze, Hummels and Lewandowski all departed for Bavaria over the next couple of seasons, bringing more glory to Munich and more heartache for Dortmund, who have not won the league since. Although Götze and Hummels would eventually return to the Westfalenstadion, Lewandowski remains in Munich, lauded as one of the best strikers in the world, smashing every Bundesliga and German football goal milestone along the way, while propelling Bayern to a quite unbelievable record of nine Bundesliga titles in a row. Is a rivalry still a rivalry when the same side comes out on top every season? Possibly not. But with such passion, entertainment and excitement on show, even only playing for pride has its place on the global stage. Football fans around the world sit up and take notice when Bayern play Dortmund. Der Klassiker is here to stay.

THE REVIERDERBY

Borussia Dortmund v Schalke

By Emma Storey and Marius Kortholt

Der Klassiker may be the Bundesliga rivalry that grabs the global headlines, but for local bragging rights, it doesn't come much fiercer than the Revierderby: Borussia Dortmund vs. Schalke. The match has been described as "the mother of all derbies" in Germany, such is the rivalry between the two clubs from the working class, industrialised Ruhr region, which dates back to 1925. The cities of Dortmund and Gelsenkirchen are separated by less than 20 miles

and there is no middle ground in this former coal and steel heartland: you're either Royal Blue or Black and Yellow.

It may surprise you to know, given recent form, that Schalke were the original kings of the Ruhr back in the pre-Bundesliga days. It took 18 years for Dortmund to record a single Revierderby victory, such was Schalke's dominance, as they won six German Championships between 1934 and 1942. But (after World War II,) it was BVB who began to dominate in the 1950s and 60s, setting the tone for the birth of the Bundesliga in 1963.

The rivals were both founding members of the league and the Revierderby soon became an unmissable fixture in the calendar. One particularly infamous incident came in September 1969. Schalke took the lead at Dortmund's Rote Erde Stadium, resulting in furious home fans storming the pitch. Police used dogs to try and control the crowds, only for one of them, a canine named Rex, to bite the bottom of Schalke defender Friedel Rausch: a moment caught on camera to become one of the most iconic photographs in German football.

Recent matches have become the stuff of legend for their unpredictability and wild comebacks for both sides, the most recent of which in 2017/18 saw Schalke fight back from 4-0 down at half time to claim a sensational draw at the Westfalenstadion. For all the drama though, there has only been one winner in the Bundesliga era: BVB have eight titles in that time while Schalke haven't won the league since 1958, a fact that no Dortmunder allows them to forget. And when Schalke should have ended that drought in 2006/07, it was Dortmund who put a stop to it, winning that season's Revierderby on the penultimate match day of the season to destroy their great rival's chance of claiming a first Bundesliga title.

THE INTER-CONTINENTAL DERBY

Fenerbahçe vs Galatasaray

Throughout this book, Eli Mengem recalls his experiences of attending derby matches across the world for COPA90's Derby Days series. His recollections begin with the story of his trip to Istanbul to learn more about the rivalry between Galatasaray SK and Fenerbahçe SK where he witnessed a match between Turkish football's 'big two'.

Turkey and in particular, Istanbul, is a brilliant place full of all kinds of wonders and wondrous people. COPA90's time there in April 2014 was made so special by the locals, whose insistent hospitality is second to none, whether it's local fishermen sharing sandwiches with us or the Galatasaray President feeding me the local delicacy himself.

But balanced with that hospitable charm, there is an anger in some Turkish people that I don't think I've ever come across

before. The smallest confrontation can turn into a punch up within seconds - something we became privy to on multiple occasions. As one interview subject we spoke to said, "In Turkey you can be at the lights and if one guy says, 'go it's green, why did you stop?' you can have a fight".

And so it's no wonder the second biggest religion behind Islam in Turkey, football, boasts such an infamously violent streak. The Istanbul derby has been blighted by injuries, even deaths, while it has other controversies on its record too. In fact, by the time we got to Turkey, due to another fan death, away fans had been banned from attending the fixture. Just like with the absence of the tifos when we visited Milan for the Derby della Madonnina, it therefore felt like we didn't get to attend a 'true' version of the fixture. That's not to say we didn't experience one hell of a matchday though...

From early morning within the city, brilliant scenes were provided by the congregational style of Turkish fandom as they sat down and then sprung up to sing and bounce around. With Istanbul's tight historic alleys and lanes, you often have no choice but to stop and watch the scenes play out on a matchday. In some streets, traffic has come to a complete stop and even walking across some thoroughfares is near impossible, due to the amount of people there to have a good time.

Galatasaray's ground, then known as the Türk Telekom Stadium, took a little too long to get to - give me the smaller, inner-city stadia any day of the week (in Istanbul, I recommend Beşiktaş' Vodafone Park Arena for those of you with similar tastes). But in getting the subway to the ground, the fans made the long, arduous journey, an incredibly joyous, stimulating one with never-ending chants and the only ever pyro I've seen pulled out on the underground!

We experienced complications with entry due to an overzealous ID card system making visits for casual supporters

The Intercontinental Derby
Galatasaray SK 1-0 Fenerbahçe SK
Süper Lig, 6th of April 2014
Türk Telekom Stadium, Istanbul, Turkey

extremely complicated. Once we got into the ground, it didn't take too long to see why this fixture is so famous the world over.

Even before kick-off, we saw that famous Turkish love of fighting - this time a punch up between two journalists! As the players came out onto the pitch, the Galatasaray fans did some kind of collective whistle, a noise so strong and

so disturbing I genuinely thought I was going to faint.

The match itself was a forgetful one, a Wesley Sneijder goal deciding it early on in Galatasaray's favour. But this fixture was never really about what was happening on the pitch – it was all about scenes around it. It was just a shame off it, we couldn't have both sets of fans present.

THE ETERNAL DERBY

FK Partizan vs Crvena zvezda

Summing up the intense animosity between supporters of FK Partizan and Crvena zvezda and the feeling that their rivalry will 'last forever', the 'Belgrade Derby' is more commonly known as the 'Eternal Derby'. Eli Mengem visited Serbia back in 2014 for a match between these great enemies for Series 1 of COPA90's Derby Days series.

I remember touching down in Belgrade and the first graffiti I saw in the city - a mural to Red Star (Crvena zvezda) Belgrade's infamous 'Delje' Ultras. As you do, I snapped a photo, added a filter and posted it on my instagram. Within minutes, the first comment I received was, "I showed this picture to my brother-in-law who lives out there and he said you won't come back alive".

Luckily, I'm still alive to tell the tale!

Belgrade is a brilliant city, full of historic wonders far beyond football. Whichever corner you turn, the rich history of the city is on full display, whether it's castles and forts from the first century or bullet-strewn buildings from much more contemporary conflicts. The point is, the consequences of aggression are omnipresent and it's no different in its footballing circles.

All around the city, graffiti related to either club was tagged with ominous imagery whether it be skulls, knives or military insignia. Even adorning the stadiums themselves, we saw street art that gave us goosebumps for all the wrong reasons. Which, funnily enough, was the exact opposite experience we had of the locals - especially in the footballing worlds where journalists and fans alike would all insist on buying us drinks, telling us tales and chatting with a fluency of English far better than anything we had come across in Italy, Spain or even Germany.

No more so was that the case than with one member of the Partizan media team, with whom I remember sharing a bizarre chat about his love of Luton Town and betting accumulators on English football. At the end of the stadium tour, he then presented us with not only free tickets, but full pitch-side access and broadcasting rights to the match to show the world the wonders of the 'Eternal Derby'.

After eight episodes where every request was met with diplomatic rejections or ignorance from the so-called 'big' clubs, it was incredible to us it was in the lesser known, poorer league, that the media department understood the significance and importance of what we were making and how it would benefit the fixture.

Despite the pleasantries, on the day of the match, I was still quite nervous. With only so many pitch-side access tickets I gave mine up to a colleague and instead attended the match in the home end with the fans, chaperoned by one of our interview subjects, Nenad - a die-hard Red Star fan. He told me his near flawless English was a result of binge watching Only Fools and Horses and following Newcastle United (he didn't want to talk about the similarity of Newcastle's black and white kit to Red Star's Belgrade rivals, Partizan!). The idea was with Nenad, I could enjoy the game stress free with someone who spoke the language and knew his way around the city and ground. But this arrangement, involving me,

meant something had to go wrong... and it did, before we even got into the ground!

Having turned up late after stopping in the middle of the city to gawk at the biggest-ever Panini sticker swap I had ever seen (the 2014 World Cup was around the corner) and then having been distracted by the procession of ultras marching through the city, we got to the ground quite late and had to rush to make it to kick-off.

Like any contentious fixture, upon entering the ground, every spectator is subject to strict pat downs and our section was no exception. In a rush and knowing I wasn't carrying anything on me, I casually approached the police expecting my pat down to be over before it started, but to my surprise within a moment's inspection they took me over to the side and started questioning me... in Serbian. I explained I didn't understand but they didn't believe me and it was only the intervention of Nenad that saved the day.

Turns out, having filmed my lines to the camera all day then having rushed into the game as we always do, I had forgotten to take off my mic lapel and the police thought I was an undercover policeman. They were trying to warn me that, if caught, I would be killed in the terraces, so it was lucky they had done their job properly!

Inside the ground, well what can I say? Not much besides the cliché words that unfortunately don't do justice to the scenes provided from both home and away fans. There was a cacophony of noise, flags, aggression, tifos and, most impressively, pyrotechnics. It felt like there must have been a military truck raided to provide the amount of light,

smoke and bombs that went off during the match, no more so than at half time when both sets of fans put on such a light show, my pupils were dilated until long after the match.

As for the game itself, we were privy to a classic. Partizan, needing a win to stay within grasp of Red Star's four-point lead at the top, didn't get off to the best of starts when they conceded a penalty early on. But the home keeper provided the heroics and saved the spot kick and not long after, Partizan took the lead. Red Star were later awarded another penalty but once again the keeper went the right way and saved. But eventually, Red Star got the ball in the net and it looked all over for Partizan not just for the match but the season at that point. That was until Nemanja Kojić scored a late winner as the black and white side of the rivalry lost their minds, with pitch invasions and limbs that rival anything I've ever seen. The game ended with the Partizan captain celebrating in his underwear under a rainbow of pyro and flags and we left knowing for season one, Derby Days had ended on the best note possible.

The Eternal Derby
FK Partizan 2-1 Crvena zvezda
Serbian SuperLiga, 26th of April 2014
Partizan Stadium, Belgrade, Serbia

REST OF THE WORLD

While Europe dominates the football world in terms of the power and financial clout of its leagues, many would argue that the best fan experiences - and most visceral passion for the sport - lie elsewhere.

For the sheer noise, colour and overall spectacle of its matchdays alone, attending a game in South America has to be considered a 'must' on every football supporter's bucket list. The continent's club rivalries are amongst the fiercest on the globe. The 'Paulista Derby' in São Paulo, Brazil - involving Sport Club Corinthians Paulista and Sociedade Esportiva Palmeiras – was once included in global broadcaster CNN's top ten list of the world's biggest football derbies, alongside a beast of a fixture from Uruguay - Peñarol versus Nacional.

Perhaps a little less well-known, but equally as fiery, the rivalry between Cerro Porteño and Club Olimpia brings Paraguay's capital Asunción to a standstill when they go head-to-head, while 'El Clásico Paisa' between Atlético Nacional and Independiente Medellín, based in Medellín, Colombia has become infamous for its violence. Argentina's main derbies include the 'Rosario Derby' between Newell's Old Boys and Rosario Central and the 'Avellaneda Derby' - Racing Club versus Independiente. But none come bigger in the country, the continent or possibly, the world, than the Superclásico between Boca Juniors and River Plate, which features overleaf.

One of the most significant derbies in Africa is the 'Cairo Derby' between Al Ahly SC and Zamalek. The two sides were named the first and second most successful African clubs of the 20th century by the Confederation of African Football (CAF), outlining the significance of their matches in the Egyptian Premier League and, indeed, when they meet in the CAF Champions League. No clubs have won either competition more than Al Ahly or Zamalek.

From North Africa to South Africa, the 'Soweto Derby' - Kaizer Chiefs versus Orlando Pirates - is another huge rivalry between two of the country's most illustrious and best-supported teams. The Tunis derby - Club Africain versus Espérance - is the biggest fixture (and rivalry) on offer in Tunisia, while the supporters of Moroccan sides Raja and Wydad produce an incredible spectacle when they clash at their shared Stade Mohammed V home.

The 'Kolkata Derby', involving East Bengal and ATK Mohun Bagan in West Bengal, India, is considered the jewel in Asia's club footballing crown. As with other derbies around the world, the rivalry between the two sets of fans is based on more than football alone. There is clear division between the supporters, with Mohun Bagan fans typically represented by people from the western part of Bengal (known as Ghotis), while East Bengal are primarily supported by people hailing from the eastern part of pre-independence Bengal (known as Bangals). Elsewhere, the 'Tehran Derby' in Iran regularly sees crowds in excess of 100,000 in attendance to see Esteghlal take on Persepolis.

A number of derbies in Japan and South Korea have their origins in company rivalries – the parent companies of Seoul's 'Super Match' between FC Seoul and Suwon Samsung Bluewings are technology giants LG Electronics and Samsung Electronics, while Japan's Osaka Derby - Cerezo Osaka versus Gamba Osaka - features clubs that were former company teams of Yanmar and Matsushita Electric Industrial (now Panasonic).

Beijing Guoan versus Shanghai Shenhua is considered the 'National Derby' of China, due in no small part to the civic power struggle between the two cities the clubs represent. Shanghai Shenhua against Shanghai Port and Guangzhou versus Guangzhou City are two of China's most fervent inner-city derbies.

Many North American club rivalries are in their infancy compared with other continents and leagues around the world. That's not to say any should be disregarded. Eli Mengem went to one of the MLS' top derbies – Portland Timbers versus Seattle Sounders - for COPA90's Derby Days and has written about "the most bona fide football culture in the country (the United States of America)" for this book. New York Red Bulls versus New York City FC only became a derby in 2015, when the latter club joined the MLS. But fans in the 'Big Apple' have quickly come to dislike one another!

Canadian clubs also compete in the MLS, and Montreal Impact against Toronto FC has gained the moniker of 'Canadian Classique' or the '401 Derby' (based on the name of the Ontario Highway 401 – the main driving route between the two cities).

THE SUPERCLÁSICO

Boca Juniors vs River Plate

"The biggest, baddest of them all" is how British football magazine FourFourTwo describes the derby clashes between Argentinian giants Boca Juniors and River Plate. Even if you aren't a fan of either team, taking a trip to Buenos Aires to watch them go head-to-head at La Bombonera or El Monumental was given the number one spot of "50 sporting things you must do before you die" by 'The Observer'.

Since the establishment of the Primera División in 1891, 71 of the 191 top-flight titles on offer in Argentina have been won by one of Buenos Aires' 'big two' - Club Atlético Boca Juniors or Club Atlético River Plate. It should be noted from the outset that between 1967 and 1985 and then between 1991 and 2014, two top-flight championships were on offer each calendar year – the Metropolitano and Nacional (1967-1985), the Apertura and Clausura (1991-2012) and the Inicial and Final (2012-2014) – hence the large number of titles the clubs have won to date.

Both Boca and River Plate have their origins in La Boca – a working class area in the south east of Buenos Aires, close to its old port. One of Buenos Aires' 48 'barrios' (neighbourhoods), it was in La Boca that River were founded in 1901, as a result of the merger of two clubs, called Santa Rosa and La Rosales. Boca were established there in 1905 by a group of boys that had been part of a team called Independencia Sud. River Plate's name comes from the English name for the city's estuary - Río de la Plata – while Boca's name combines the name of the barrios they are from with the English word, 'Juniors'. It was common for Argentinian teams of the day to incorporate English words as British railway workers had originally introduced football into Argentina.

The sides first met in a friendly match on the 2nd of August 1908. Records from that game are sparse but it is understood that Boca won 2-1. A year later, River

joined the Primera División, finishing second in the 10-team league in their debut top-flight season. Boca joined them in 1913, with River winning 2-1 in the first competitive match between the clubs, staged at Racing Club Stadium on the 24th of August that year.

Boca gained greater success in their early decades in the Primera División, winning six titles between 1919 and 1930 compared to River's solitary triumph in 1920. River opted to move away from La Boca barrios in 1923, moving to the Alvear y Tagle in the Recoleta district of Buenos Aires. They then moved again in 1938 to their current home, the Estadio

Monumental, in the affluent district of Núñez in the north of the city.

River had gained the nickname of Los Millonarios (the Millionaires) by that point in their history following the expensive signings of players such as Carlos Peucelle from Sportivo Buenos Aires in 1931 and Bernabé Ferreyra from Tigre in 1932. Playing in such wealthy surroundings as Núñez only enhanced this 'Millonarios' tag. In comparison, Boca stayed true to their roots, building their current ground – La Bombonera (the Chocolate Box) – in their home barrios between 1938 and 1940.

Boca's roots continue to play a key part in the club's identity. Their fanbase are known as 'Los Xeneizes' (the Genoese – as spelt in Genose dialect) after the Italian immigrants from Genoa who co-founded the team with a group of Greek boys on the 3rd of April 1905. Boca Juniors fans are also known as 'Los Bosteros' (the manure handlers) – a term that originates from the use of horse manure at a brick factory on the site where La Bombonera now stands. It has been common for supporters – even players – from rival clubs to hold their nose in reference to this as a means of insulting Boca fans. On the same theme, Boca fans are also called 'Los Chanchitos' ('Little Pigs') while Boca supporters called their River adversaries 'Gallinas' ('Chickens') after their side's defeat to Peñarol in the 1966 Copa Libertadores Final. River's players were accused of lacking guts against their Uruguayan opponents and the slur stuck.

It is the clubs' identities that lie at the heart of the Boca-River rivalry. A divide has been drawn along class lines, with Boca portrayed as a working-class club that is proud of its immigrant and barrios roots, while River are said to be the team of the upper-middle class. These are huge generalisations of course and, increasingly, untrue with both clubs attracting support across all demographics in Buenos Aires and beyond.

River's departure from the La Boca barrios lit the touch paper on a rivalry which dominates Argentinian football to date. A report from a Boca-River match in 1931, which was eventually called off only 30 minutes in, describes police on horseback attempting to quell pitch invasions and scuffles between the two sets of supporters. Between 1931 and 1937, Boca and River won eight of the ten Primera División titles, as both teams' popularity extended well beyond Buenos Aires. The demographics of their supporter bases changed considerably as a result, yet the old notion of a class divide persists.

Both clubs have enjoyed glorious periods in their history. Under the management of Renato Cesarini and then Carlos Peucelle, River Plate were given the nickname 'La Maquina' (the Machine) by journalist Ricardo Lorenzo in El Gráfico sports newspaper after he had watched them demolish Chacarita Juniors 6-2 on 12 June 1942. River had a legendary forward line of Juan Carlos Muñoz, José Manuel Moreno, Adolfo Pedernera, Ángel Labruna and Félix Loustau and between 1941 and 1947, won four Primera División leagues and three Copa Aldaos. Peucelle, who had played in the early 'La Maquina', handed a professional debut to the world-renowned Alfredo Di Stéfano in 1945. This side later developed another nickname – 'Caballeros de la Angustia' (Knights of Anguish) – due to the way they would overwhelm their opponents.

Boca won back-to-back Copa Libertadores in 1977 and 1978 but many consider their greatest team of all-time to be the all-conquering side of the early to mid-2000s under the management of Carlos Bianchi. Los Xeneizes won the 1998 Apertura, 1999 Clausura and 2000 Apertura with Bianchi at the helm and boasting star players such as Juan Román Riquelme and Martín Palermo. National success was replicated on a continental stage as they lifted the Copa Libertadores in 2000, 2001 and 2003. The latter success saw Bianchi become the first manager to win four Copa Libertadores, having also claimed the trophy during his time in charge of Vélez Sarsfield. Boca eliminated River en route to winning the competition in 2000 and also beat them in 2004.

There is also division between the two sets of supporters in terms of their footballing philosophy. River fans expect attractive football and urge the values of the 'Three G's' on their players: 'Gustar' (to play well), 'Ganar' (to win), 'Golear' (to score goals). Boca on the other hand are all about the 'Garrar' (the claw). They expect their players to put in 100% effort and win, no matter what it takes.

It is not known for sure when the term Superclásico was first applied to a Boca-River fixture, but it is understood that the Spanish word clásico – meaning 'classic' and the closest equivalent to the English term 'derby' – was first used in Argentina before then in relation to other fixtures such as Barcelona-Real Madrid and the Mexican derby between América and Guadalajara.

What makes the Boca-River rivalry special is there is very little between the two sides in terms of trophy haul. River have won the Primera División 37 times to Boca's 34 at the time of writing, while the Los Xeneizes have been more successful than Los Millonarios in the Copa Libertadores with six successes in that competition to River's four.

The 2000 Intercontinental Cup saw Boca beat a Real Madrid side containing players such as Roberto Carlos, Luís Figo and Raúl while they also overcame AC Milan and the likes of Paolo Maldini, Andrea Pirlo and Clarence Seedorf in the 2003 edition. To date, Boca have won three Intercontinental Cups (1977, 2000, 2003) to River's one (won in 1986).

While River have collected seven Primera División titles and two Copa Libertadores since 2000, the club also suffered the indignity of their first-ever relegation in 2011 – although they bounced straight back to the top division the following season. Boca have won 10 titles and four Copa Libertadores in the same timeframe, but with River having won the most recent Primera División at the time of writing this book – as well as the 2018 Copa Libertadores Final between the two sides – the rivals are as closely matched as ever. There has rarely been much between Boca and River throughout history either. As well as having a similar trophy tally, after 256 clashes in all competitions, Boca have won 89 games to River's 84, while there have been 83 draws.

The fixture has produced many memorable moments, such as Severino Varela's diving header for Boca en route to a 2-1 victory over River and the Primera División title in 1943. On the 14th of

December 1969, Boca came from two goals down to draw 2-2 with River at El Monumental to claim the title on their rivals' home turf while River managed the same feat with a 3-0 win at La Bombonera in December 1994. Twenty years later, River defeated Boca 1–0 at El Monumental in the second leg of the 2014 Copa Sudamericana semi-finals. In addition to their goal from Leonardo Pisculichi, the game was also memorable for goalkeeper Marcelo Barovero's penalty save early in the match.

For all its great moments, sadly the Superclásico has also had its fair share of shameful incidents too. The second leg of a Copa Libertadores round of 16 tie had to be abandoned at half time in 2015 when Boca supporters attacked River players with pepper spray. Boca were disqualified from the tournament while River went on to win the competition for the first time since 1996.

Worse still was an incident after a goalless draw between the two sides at El Monumental on the 23rd of June 1968. A crush at gate 12 at the stadium led to the death of 71 Boca fans, with the average age of the victims just 19. Some claim the disaster came as a result of Boca fans throwing lit River flags from the upper tiers of the stadium, causing a stampede of their own fans in the lower tier. Others say River fans arrived at the Boca section, causing the stampede, while further accounts point at police brutality. After three years of investigation, a government inquiry didn't level culpability at anyone for the disaster.

There were also ugly scenes when Boca and River met in the ultimate Superclásico: the 2018 Copa Libertadores Final. The New York Times billed the fixture as "The Final to end all Finals" while AS Argentina described it as the "most important final in Argentina's football history". In the last-ever two-legged final, River Plate perhaps had the slight advantage after the first leg, gaining a 2-2 draw at Boca's La Bombonera. Then, prior to the second leg of the final on the 24th of November 2018, Boca's team bus was attacked en route to the Estadio Monumental. Multiple players were injured as a result of the broken

"The on-pitch atmosphere reflects the 2,000 policemen that patrol the stadium: bust-ups, red cards (two per game is common) and controversy are part of the derby.

Attending a Boca-River game, especially at La Bombonera, is a once-in-a-lifetime experience. In the stands you can expect anything – from chicken feathers to flying pigs"

- FourFourTwo

glass and pepper spray attack. The match kick-off time was changed four times before eventually being postponed for 24 hours. The following day, CONMEBOL - South American football's governing body – agreed to postpone the match once again at the request of Boca Juniors. In an unprecedented move, it was eventually decided that the second leg not only be played outside Argentina but outside South America due to safety concerns. On the 29th of November 2018, CONMEBOL confirmed the game would be played at Real Madrid's Santiago Bernabéu ground on the 9th of December 2018.

River eventually triumphed 3-1 after extra-time in front of over 60,000 fans in the Spanish capital. Reuters' Richard Martin wrote in his match report that River's win "guarantees them bragging rights over their neighbours for many years to come".

While River fans can always boast that victory of victories, both sets of supporters know that in a rivalry as hotly contested as Boca-River it is always the destination of the next trophy and, in particular, the result of the next Superclásico that matters most.

THE CASCADIA DERBY

Portland Timbers vs Seattle Sounders

Eli Mengem ventured to Oregon to discover one of the MLS' most heated rivalries. Along with Vancouver Whitecapes, Portland Timbers and Seattle Sounders compete for the fan-created Cascadia Cup, which is awarded each season to the best team in the Pacific Northwest.

In 2015, Derby Days left Europe for the first time and despite the many rivalries on offer across Africa, South America and Asia, with the rapid rise of the MLS during the time, it was fitting we took the first alternative episode to the new world of 'Soccer in the States'.

The derby between Seattle Sounders and Portland Timbers is known as the 'Cascadia Derby' - Cascadia being the name of the unofficial region of the rain soaked, pine tree covered North West America. It's an area I've always been obsessed with thanks to its significant role in pop culture from music (Sub Pop Records, Nirvana) to films (One Flew Over The Cuckoo's Nest, almost all of Gus Van Sant's early work).

The region is also home to the most bona fide football culture in the country, where despite both clubs having, at the time, only played in the MLS for the past half decade, their origins and

rivalry go all the way back to the North American Soccer League (NASL) in the 1970s.

The elements that underpin this rivalry make it truly unique. Whilst the dislike fans feel towards one another is legitimate, with both cities being havens of progressive politics, culture and lifestyles, there is mutual respect, if not appreciation. Therefore, this is very much a rivalry born purely out of football and the desire to prove who has a more football-mad city/club. It's very much open to debate which city/club that is!

Seattle has the bigger crowds, averaging an incredible 40,000 but it also has a bigger population and stadium. Portland is a far more tight-knit city, where sport is omnipresent all around town. The city boasts some of the best crowds - not just in the MLS but in college soccer and with their women's team, the Portland Thorns.

The style of support in Portland was fascinating to experience - a brilliant combination of American and European styles. There was the Timbers' incredible 'supporters house', inspired by the German fanhousen. The tifo displays from both sides were genuinely as impressive as any I've seen in Europe. Then there was the incredible stake out, which saw

The Cascadia Derby
Portland Timbers 4-1 Seattle Sounders
MLS, 28th of June 2015
Providence Park, Portland, United States

the Portland fans sleep out overnight outside the ground to get the best seat in the active supporter area as that section of the ground worked on a first in, first-served basis.

The game, a 4-1 rout to the hosts, whilst perhaps not as chaotic as European/South American matchdays, was nonetheless a festival of noise and colour. Smoke bombs were safely positioned on the front of the terrace and timed to go off after goals and cheesy bounce-alongs hardly had the ominous doom I'd experienced in Sarajevo. But it was also brilliantly unique and a sign that the USA is forging its own style of active support that relates to its soccer community. No more so was this the case than the plethora of rainbow flags in both ends of the ground at this match - something still rare in Europe today.

Other Titles in this Aspen Books Series include:

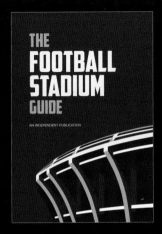

www.aspenbooks.co.uk